Abortion and Martyrdom

Abortion and Martyrdom

The Papers of the Solesmes Consultation and an Appeal to the Catholic Church

Edited by

Aidan Nichols, O.P.

GRACEWING

First published in 2002

Gracewing
2 Southern Avenue, Leominster
Herefordshire HR6 0QF

NIHIL OBSTAT   Monsignor Gerald Chidgey, J. C. D. Censor

IMPRIMATUR   Most Revd. Peter Smith, Ll.B., J. C. D.
                           Archbishop of Cardiff

Date   7 December 2001

The *Nihil Obstat* and *Imprimatur* are official declarations that a book or pamphlet is free of doctrinal error. No implication is contained therein that those who have granted the *Nihil Obstat* and *Imprimatur* necessarily recommend or endorse the book or pamphlet.

UK ISBN 0 85244 543 1

Typesetting by Action Publishing Technology Ltd,
Gloucester, GL1 5SR

Printed in England by
MPG Books Ltd.,
Bodmin PL31 1EG

Contents

Abbreviations

AAS	*Acta Apostolicae Sedis* (Rome: Vatican Polyglot Press, 1909–)
CCC	*The Catechism of the Catholic Church* (Et London: Chapman 1994)
DH	P. Hünermann (ed.), *Heinrich Denzinger, Enchiridion symbolorum, definitionum et declarationum de rebus fidei et morum* (Freiburg: Herder, 1991)
DTC	A. Vacant, E. Mangenot, E. Amann (eds.), *Dictionnaire de Théologie catholique* (Paris: Letouzey et Ané, 1909–1950)
In Sent.	*Scriptum super librum Sententiarum*
PG	*Patrologia Graeca*, ed. J.-P. Migne (Paris: Garnier et Migne, 1857–1866)
PL	*Patrologia Latina*, ed. J.-P. Migne (Paris: Garnier et Migne, 1844–1864)
ST	*Summa Theologiae*

Note on Contributors

Hugh Barbour is Prior of St Michael's Abbey, Orange

Denis Biju-Duval is Professor of Pastoral Theology at the Lateran University

Brian Harrison is Professor of Moral Theology at the Catholic University of Puerto Rico

Philippe Jobert is Professor of Dogmatic Theology at the Abbey of S. Pierre de Solesmes

Peter Kwasniewski is Instructor in Philosophy at the International Theological Institute for Studies on Marriage and Family at Gaming, Austria

John. F. McCarthy is *Capo Ufficio* in the Roman Congregation for the Eastern Churches

Aidan Nichols is Prior of Blackfriars, Cambridge

John Saward is G. K. Chesterton Fellow at Plater College, Oxford

Michele M. Schumacher is *collaboratrice scientifique externe* in the Faculty of Theology of the University of Fribourg

Introduction

Aidan Nichols, O.P.

The objection of Catholic Christianity to the practice of abortion is well-known. Of the various evils that afflict human society in our time, the murder of defenceless children in the womb is the most gross. The arguments Catholics deploy in the effort to convince their opponents, or the undecided, of the intrinsic evil of abortion are drawn – quite properly – from rational ethics. By appeal to the moral reason, as it works on data generally accessible to any reflective person, it should be possible to show that the destruction of human lives guiltless of any offence save that of existing is an anti-humane act of peculiar, indeed unique, virulence – in a word, that abortion is *wrong*.

The matter does not, however, end there. The passion which Catholics and other 'pro-life' representatives, whether Christian or not, bring to this cause derives in part from the rational humanism they share – or so they hope – with their fellow citizens in civil society. That is the basis of the dialogue to which they are committed. But that passion can also derive from a biblical imperative: for the Judaeo-Christian Scriptures place especial emphasis on the divine favour toward the weakest and most vulnerable members of creation, and see in their defence and vindication (compare the ideas of salvation and redemption) a God-like duty or task.

The special status of aborted children as at one and the same time personal innocents and defenceless victims has to be theologically significant. Perhaps, unknown to the present writer, theologians here and there are already turning their minds to the question of the soteriological particularity of such children – the special niche they may inhabit in the divine plan of salvation for the world. Could Catholicism, which already venerates as blood-witnesses to revelation the Jewish babes of Bethlehem, massacred in place of Christ, affirm of these children that they too died in silent testimony to a truth greater than themselves – in their case, the truth of the divine command, 'Thou shalt not kill': thou shalt not destroy innocent life?

In the late summer of 1999, Dom Philippe Dupont, the Abbot of Solesmes graciously hosted a modest 'Consultation' where the theological bases, and inconveniences, of this proposal might be addressed. It was not a condition of participation that speakers should take one side of this disputed question. Perusal of the papers now published in book form will soon show how diverse were the opinions presented – though all fall within the bounds of accepted theological discussion in the Catholic Church.

The Consultation, chaired by the editor of this study, consisted, it may be said, of maximalists and minimalists: those who wished theology, and the Church, to acknowledge the largest possible number of the aborted (perhaps all) as recipients of the 'Baptism of blood', and those who considered this thesis temerarious, and were willing to consider as candidates for such recognition only a tiny minority of cases. The Agreed Statement, in seeking to express a consensus position of those present, naturally tends to a more limited thesis on which moral unanimity was possible. (It was regretted by all present that Dom Philippe Jobert, professor of dogmatics at Solesmes and moving spirit of the Consultation, felt unable to sign the Statement for this reason.) It may be observed here that even this 'limited' thesis, fully in accord with classical theological positions as it is, will, however, surprise many, both inside and outside the Church. A more generous application of the key principles can be found in the 'supplementary theses' which participants were able to support as possibly (and so not certainly) true articulations of Catholic faith.

A particular – and unexpected – difficulty in our deliberations concerned the question of the moment of ensoulment, a topic on which, at least in the judgment of some present, the Church has not yet fully clarified her mind. (Others take a different view of the burden, and intentions, of the magisterial documents already in place.) That issue was unavoidable inasmuch as any attempt to secure the declaration of the martyr status of particular aborted infants will need to bear in mind the quantity of time that has passed since their conception. The problem of finding a suitable formulation on this point explains other absences from the list of signatories to the Statement whose names may be found, however, as sources for the supplementary theses.

On the feast of the Presentation, the last feast of the Christmas cycle, in the year 2000, both Statement and theses were sent to a variety of Bishops' Conferences around the world, as well as to several dicasteries of the Holy See. The Cardinal President of the Pontifical Council for the Family, Archbishop Alfonso López Trujillo, in his reply, expressed the desire to see further theological discussion of these issues. This collection of essays, which I place under the patronage of the Babe of Bethlehem and the Holy Innocents, is intended to serve that end.

Blackfriars, Cambridge,
Memorial day of St Paulinus of York, 2001

1

Setting the question

Philippe Jobert, O.S.B., Abbey of Saint-Pierre de Solesmes and Aidan Nichols, O.P., Blackfriars, Cambridge

Can the Magisterium of the Church acknowledge children killed in abortion as 'companions of the Holy Innocents' (and therefore martyrs)?

It is a commonplace of Catholic theology that infants, even in the womb, who are killed from *odium fidei*, 'hatred of the faith', may be regarded as having undergone a 'Baptism of blood'. The question we wish to raise is whether it is possible and desirable to regard all aborted children, without exception, as supernaturally included within the embrace of divine redemption, to the point, indeed, that the Church, by a solemn act, could declare publicly their martyr status, and invite their intercession.

A 'culture of death' (John Paul II) is a pattern of assumptions and attitudes, found in both the sensibilities of individual persons and the structures of corporate institutions in civil society, the effect of which is to render parents, doctors and lawmakers insensitive to the sacred dignity of human life – especially unborn human life in its mother's womb. Such life, like all human life, already embodies, through the act of creation, the image of God, but it is a specifying feature of the unborn that they have not, as yet, sullied that image by any act of personal sin. True, the nature in which they are created no longer enjoys the communion with God which Adamic grace gave the proto-parents, and suffers that inner dislocation which is the consequence of this deprivation. Affected by original sin, their natural will is not directed to supernatural life. Yet though the divine creative act does not, simply as such, incorporate the newly conceived within the supernatural order of healing and elevation to share the vision of the Holy Trinity, it is nonetheless the design of the divine mercy to order all human beings to that wondrous end. It will be attained – in every case where human freedom meets grace and does not oppose it – by the application of the all-sufficient merits of the Word incarnate in his atoning Cross ('the Blood') through the gift of Baptism ('the water') whether in the sacramental waters or in the 'Baptism of desire' or 'of blood'.

The question of the 'Baptism of blood' arises in the case of aborted infants since their deaths give witness to the word of God, 'You shall not kill', a word written in the conscience of every human being (cf. Rom. 2, 15), so therefore in the murderer's soul. Their murders prevent God from giving justification through Baptism, the ordinary way of salvation in the Christian era. The personal sinlessness of the unborn and their ordering, in the divine intention, to grace and glory renders them, it may be thought, an object of predilection for the malice of the evil Angels whose activity assists the formation of a 'culture of death' operating with especial intensity in the practice of abortion. Hence *odium fidei* is at work not only in human intentions originated so as deliberately to express such hatred, but at the transcendent level of angelic causality ('the Dragon' of the Apocalypse).

In such a context, aborted infants are brought to their deaths by the same 'rulers of this age' (I Cor. 2:8), who crucified Jesus, and constitute, indeed, icons of his 'crucified Innocence'. In his divine justice, exercised towards all human beings, will not God give these children – whose death is not only a natural but also and above all a supernatural injustice – the supernatural justice he wills for all? Though aborted infants are distinguished from the Holy Innocents whom the Liturgy of the Church commemorates at Christmas in that they were not first aggregated to the people of God by an outward sign (circumcision) typifying Baptism, nor did they die in place of Jesus, nevertheless their combination of personal guiltlessness and the ordering of their humanity to share the Father's glory through Christ conforms them inchoately to the image of the Son, while their violent deaths at the behest (human or angelic) of those who despise the divine image in man, render them more specifically isomorphic with the Son in his crucified condition. Like all martyrs, the aborted point to Jesus in the mystery of his rejection and humiliation. 'Virgin martyrs' are evangelical signs of holiness.

These aborted infants may be held to stand in a special relation also to the Mother of God whose appointment to be Mother of the Church (John 19: 26–27) is inseparable from the compassion she showed at the cross when the 'sword' of Simeon's prophecy pierced her soul (Luke 2: 35). The spiritual ('hidden and mystical') wounds with which the Mother of Christ was afflicted on Calvary when she too 'died', inwardly, in the death of the Fruit of her womb, have power to succour – in proportion (if Mary's Motherhood of the Church be the measuring-rule of her active compassion) to the depth of human need. And of all the needy, those about to be aborted – already potential members of the Church – are the weakest and most abandoned. It is through her wounded Motherhood that Mary is united in a particular mode to these children.

But if aborted children enjoy a special place within the range of Mary's spiritual Motherhood, the Church, of which the compassionate Mother of God is the exemplar, must likewise have a special regard for these infants. Their recognition as martyrs by a possible future act of the College of bishops *sub et cum Petro*, 'under and with Peter', would testify in striking fashion to the universality of the Catholic Church's philanthropic outreach in the perspective of salvation, and constitute a flaming witness to her stand in defence of the human dignity and rights of the *conceptus*, the conceived person, everywhere (*Catechism of the Catholic Church*, no. 2270). As with all those who, through glorification in Christ, have the capacity to sub-mediate the fruits of his redemption, we could expect such a 'claim' of such holy persons for the Church to be divinely answered by the bestowal of spiritual fruit. Such fruit might take the form of their powerful intercession to convert others and bring to repentance – a John the Baptist role as forerunners of the final triumph of divine Innocence. This 'Baptistine' mission would consist in eliciting, among the Church's members generally (whether actual or potential) sorrow for sins against innocence, and among parents in particular, sorrow for abortions committed or colluded in.

The 'claiming' of such children must be related not only to renewed repentance in the Holy Spirit, but also to petition for the diffusion, through the Spirit's gift, of the ethos of the Holy Family, for the supernatural environment of the Holy Family, ('the school of Nazareth' – Paul VI) teaches how 'heaven wishes families to live'. Mary and Joseph provide, through their relation with Jesus, models of care and guardianship for biological parents, and indeed for the analogues of such parents that are celibate women and men in their roles as providers of motherly and fatherly nurturing. Wherever, through the grace of the Sacred Infancy, childlike innocence exists, Christians above all must defend it, for it is a sign of entry into the Kingdom (Matt. 19: 13–15, and parallels), and a presence of the life of Christ in the world. The Holy Family is not simply a moral exemplar but a mysterious presence of the Holy Trinity – through Joseph, 'shadow' of the Father, Jesus, the Son, and Mary who is abidingly under the 'wing' of the Holy Spirit. The Holy Family is a kind of sacrament of the Trinitarian *communio*, the divine Trinity, on earth.

Is it, then, by an implicit reference to the intercessory power of the martyrs that Pope John Paul II can speak, in *Evangelium Vitae* 99, of the mothers of aborted children being 'able to ask forgiveness' from their children, who are 'now living in the Lord'? If so, these will be martyr Companions of the Holy Innocents, delighting to restore, through the grace of Christ, the dignity of offended motherhood in families made to the image of the Blessed Trinity itself.

Editor's Note:
Readers should know that the version of *Evangelium Vitae* 99 published in the official journal of the Holy See, *Acta Apostolicae Sedis*, softens the sense of this passage, replacing the statement that 'nothing is definitively lost' and the encouragement to 'ask forgiveness from your child who is now living in the Lord' with the assurance that the child can be 'entrust[ed] with sure hope' to 'the Father and his mercy'. Both versions, however, enjoy validity and can be cited as authoritative in argument, even though the Latin text of the *Acta* is the more definitive. The original English vernacular text of *Evangelium Vitae* 99 is made use of by a number of the contributors to this volume.

2

On whether aborted children should be claimed as members of the Church

John F. McCarthy
Congregation for the Eastern Churches, Rome

Introduction

For some time now voices have been heard calling upon the Catholic Church to claim all aborted children unto herself as her members baptized in the Blood of Christ. These voices say that the Church as a whole, and the Pope in particular, have the power and authority to recognize aborted children as companion martyrs of the Holy Innocents. Some are convinced that an official claiming by the Church would 'cast out the demon of abortion by invoking the Holy Spirit' upon these children and thus, in some way, 'give supernatural life to millions of human beings who, like Naaman the Syrian in 2 (4) Kings 5, did not know the true God and yet could become objects of his merciful love.' Thus also, they say, such a declaration would be a step towards healing the 'moral leprosy' of abortion in millions of its perpetrators by inviting the guilty to acts of repentance and by helping to assuage the wound of injustice felt by the victims.[1] The following is a theological reflection upon some aspects of this appeal.

The principal theological question in this appeal regards the affirmation that the Roman pontiff as supreme Pastor has the authority to proclaim aborted children to be members of the Church and companion martyrs of the first Holy Innocents. Problems inherent in this question gravitate around the necessity of Baptism in order to be saved and the necessity of having been killed as a witness of Christ in order to be a martyr. I shall here attempt to address these two problems on a theological level.

The Limbo of children

First of all, as is obvious, a fetus must be human in order to be a valid subject of Baptism or of martyrdom, and, in recent years especially, the Church has been proclaiming clearly the human character of the human fetus from the first moment of fertilization of the ovum. Thus states paragraph no. 2270 of the *Catechism of the Catholic Church*: 'Human life must be respected and protected absolutely from the moment of conception. From the first moment of his existence, a human being must be recognized as having the rights of a person – among which is the inviolable right of every innocent being to life.'[2] Throughout its history, the Catholic Church 'has affirmed the moral evil of every procured abortion' (*CCC*, no. 2271), because the human fetus was always known to be at least *aimed at* becoming a human being. But it is now known with certainty and taught by the Church that the human fetus *is* a human being from the first moment of its biological conception.[3] And so the human fetus, from the first moment of its conception, has an imperishable human soul, and it is called by God to eternal life in heaven (cf. *CCC*, no. 1703).

Aborted children die without Baptism of water. Nevertheless, the *Catechism of the Catholic Church* (no. 1261) affirms: 'As regards *children who have died without Baptism*, the Church can only entrust them to the mercy of God, as she does in her funeral rites for them. Indeed, the great mercy of God, who desires that all men should be saved, and Jesus' tenderness towards children which caused him to say: "Let the children come to me, do not hinder them" (Mark 10:14), allow us to hope that there is a way of salvation for children who have died without Baptism.' Hence, the theological problem before us in this case is whether a definite way of salvation can be indicated for the immortal souls of the victims of abortion. If they are not eventually to be brought to Heaven, where do they go?

An alternative often conjectured in the past by theologians has been that they go to Limbo. Thus Louis LaRavoire Morrow, Bishop of Krishnagar:

> Since infants who die unbaptized have committed no sins, they live in a place of *natural happiness* called 'limbo' ... Although in limbo infants enjoy complete natural happiness surpassing any on earth, such happiness cannot compare with the bliss of heaven, where souls see God face to face.[4]

Again, in a Catholic dictionary:

The Limbo of Children. It is of faith that all, children and adults, who leave this world without the Baptism of water, blood or desire and therefore in original sin are excluded from the vision of God in Heaven. The great majority of theologians teach that such children and unbaptized adults free from grievous actual sin enjoy eternally a state of perfect natural happiness, knowing and loving God by the use of their natural powers. This place and state is commonly called Limbo.[5]

A more contemporary statement is given by Lawler, Wuerl, and Lawler in their catechism for adults:

Most theologians, following St Thomas, have taught that such infants will certainly not have any personal suffering after death, and that, although they will be deprived of the blessed vision of God because they have died without grace, God will bless them with natural happiness. The Church has never made any official pronouncement on the reality or nature of limbo: but it does teach that baptism in some form is required for salvation. Many contemporary scholars have suggested that God will provide for the eternal salvation of these persons, enabling them in some way to obtain grace by a baptism of desire before death. Revelation does not give any certainty on this point.[6]

Thus we see that, while, on the one hand, the Church has never officially pronounced on 'the reality or nature of Limbo', on the other hand, the *Catechism of the Catholic Church* allows us to hope that 'there is a way of salvation for children who have died without Baptism'. Now, our specific question does not regard children in general, but children who have been lethally assaulted by abortion, and it is the contention of some that these children have received Baptism of blood, that they have been washed clean in the Blood of Christ.

The cleansing Blood of Christ

The cause of our redemption and of the efficacy of the sacrament of Baptism is the pouring out of the Blood of Jesus on the Cross, his sacrificial offering of himself to the Father on Calvary. Jesus was 'baptized' in this sense by the suffering and death that he underwent: 'I have a baptism wherewith I am to be baptized, and how I am straightened until it be accomplished' (Luke 12:50). In a related sense, all who are baptized, whether by water, blood, or desire, are washed thereby in the sacrificial Blood of Jesus: 'Blessed are they that wash their robes in the blood of the Lamb: that they may have a right to the tree of life and may enter in by the gates into the city' (Rev. 22:14). But those who have 'washed their robes' (purified their souls) through Baptism of blood have also mingled their own blood with the sanctifying Blood of Jesus; they have been graced by 'the sprinkling of blood which speaks better than that of Abel' (Heb. 12:24), precisely because it is the redemptive Blood of Christ. Have all aborted children received this Baptism of blood? Does the blood of these babies, murdered by one or both of their own parents, cry out to God from the earth as did the blood of Abel, murdered by his brother Cain (Gen. 4:10)? There are indications that it does.

When Jesus spoke of the 'baptism' wherewith he was to be baptized, he went on to say: 'Do you think that I am come to give peace on earth? I tell you, no, but separation ... The father shall be divided against the son, and the daughter against the mother ...' (Luke 12:51–53). What a great separation it is that mothers and fathers should snuff out the life of their sons and daughters while they are still in the womb! And what great occasion is thereby given to the souls of aborted children to resent this injustice! St John the Evangelist 'saw under the altar the souls of them that were slain for the word of God, and for the testimony which they held. And they cried out with a loud voice, saying: How long, O Lord, holy and true, do you not judge and revenge our blood on them that dwell on the earth?' (Rev. 6:9–10). If aborted children have in some way been killed because of Jesus and his teaching, they qualify to be among those souls 'that were slain for the word of God.'

John the Baptist died as a martyr in witness to the moral truth that adultery is contrary to the Sixth Commandment of the Law of God (Matt. 14:4 and parallels). In relation to this, St Thomas Aquinas asks whether faith alone is the cause of martyrdom. He holds that it is not. He quotes Matthew 5:10, which reads: 'Blessed are those who suffer persecution for justice's sake', which text, he explains, 'pertains to martyrdom, as the Gloss [the main mediaeval multi-author commentary on Scripture] says'. But, he adds, 'to justice pertains not only faith but also the other virtues, and, therefore, the other virtues can be the cause of martyrdom.' He goes on to say that martyrs are witnesses of Christ, so 'the truth of faith is the cause of every martyrdom.' But exterior witness is needed in addition to belief in one's heart.

> Consequently, all the virtues in their performance, according as they are referred to God, are declarations of faith through which it is made known to us that God requires works of this kind from us and rewards us for them. And in this respect they can be the cause of martyrdom. And so the martyrdom of John the Baptist is also celebrated in the Church, even though he underwent death, not in favour of the faith that was being denied, but as a reproof of adultery.[7]

Aborted children die in violation of the Fifth Commandment: 'Thou shalt not kill.' They are silent witnesses to their own right as human persons to life, liberty, and the pursuit of happiness in Heaven. Satan hates them for this witness. They are also witnesses to the obligation of their parents to protect and nurture them. Are not parents who would abrogate to the point of murder their duty towards their innocent unborn children directly resisting the teaching of Jesus about the Law of God? Does not this desire to violate a basic instinct of nature come ultimately from diabolical suggestion in the minds of the parents and in the permissiveness of society? It seems in the final analysis that the knife or drug of the abortionist is aimed ultimately at the Person of Jesus himself.

The seed of the woman

A clue to this ultimate Satanic aim may be found in Apocalypse 12, which speaks of a great sign that appeared in heaven: 'a woman clothed with the sun', who, 'being with child ... cried out in her pangs of birth, with anguish for delivery' (vv. 1–2). Now, the 'Dragon', who is Satan (v. 9), 'stood before the woman who was ready to be delivered', so that 'when she should be delivered, he might devour her son' (v. 4). This woman is the Blessed Virgin Mary, and her Son is Jesus.[8] But the Dragon did not succeed in devouring the Infant Jesus, and so, in his anger against the Woman, he 'went to make war with the rest of her seed, who keep the commandments of God and have the testimony of Jesus Christ' (vv. 16–7). 'The rest of her seed' are in one sense the spiritual children of Mary and in another sense the spiritual children of the Church. In the 'Proto-Gospel' of Genesis 3:15, the Lord God is quoted as having said to the Serpent, who is Satan: 'I will put enmity between you and the woman, and between your seed and her seed.' The enmity of Satan is understood as being directed against the divine Child of Mary in particular and against all the spiritual children of Mary and of the Church in general.[9] The question is whether aborted children do or do not become children of Mary and of the Church by the very circumstances of their death.

We know from the Gospels and from the whole of the New Testament the enmity that Satan and his seed bear against Jesus Christ and against all the loyal members of his Church. And we know from history, as well as from personal experience, the enmity that Satan with his followers bears for all those conceived by women. We know too that among the seed of Satan are to be included, not only the fallen Angels, but also those human beings who freely put themselves at the service of Satan. In that sense, those who commit abortion are acting as free instruments of Satan, who is the principal agent in these acts of murder, and who is both 'a liar' and 'a murderer from the beginning' (John 8:44). Hence, it was principally the hatred of Satan for Jesus and Mary (Gen. 3:15) as well as for all of the children of Eve that sent Herod's soldiers to kill the Holy Innocents, and those murdered children are holy because they have been bathed in the Blood of Christ. The circumstances of their death have made them members of the Church of Christ, children of God and children of Mary. Thus, the dagger of Satan did not prevent their ascent to Heaven.

That a wilfully aborting woman makes herself the seed of Satan may be inferred from Genesis 3:10: 'To the woman also [the Lord God] said: I will multiply your sorrows and your conceptions. In sorrow shall you bring forth children ...' (Douay-Rheims translation). The Revised Standard Version more freely renders these same words of the Hebrew text: 'I will greatly multiply your pain in childbearing; in pain you shall bring forth children ...' So women can be tempted for selfish reasons of comfort and convenience to exclude the bearing of children, which leads St Paul to point out: 'Adam was not seduced, but the woman, being seduced, was in the transgression. Yet, she shall be saved through childbearing, if she continue in faith and love, and sanctification, with sobriety' (1 Tim. 2:14–15).

It may be inferred from these inspired words that a woman who deliberately destroys her child is being seduced by Satan, who hates the seed of woman (Gen. 3:15), in turn to hate and kill her own seed in a Satanic war against all the physical descendants of the first Eve, but above all against the spiritual descendants of Mary, the New Eve, supernatural Mother of all the supernaturally living.

Her Son, Jesus, will crush the head of the Serpent at the end of the very same war.[10] In other words, pregnant women who refuse to give birth to the children conceived in their wombs are rejecting the Cross of Jesus and are somehow acting from hatred of the Birth of Jesus, as that is predicted in Genesis 3:15.

Martyrs are by name 'witnesses', and the Holy Innocents are recognized to be martyrs. Yet they died too young to have worshipped God or to have believed in their minds the teaching of Christ. How, then, *did* they give witness? In the opening prayer of the Mass for their feast day (December 28), the Church declares: 'Father, the Holy Innocents offered you praise by the death they suffered for Christ ...' and in the prayer after Communion: 'Lord, by a wordless profession of faith in your Son, the innocents were crowned with life at his birth ...' And likewise we hear in the entrance antiphon: 'These innocent children were slain for Christ. They follow the spotless Lamb, and proclaim for ever: Glory to you, Lord.' It is this kind of witness that is being attributed to children slaughtered by abortion, because the fact of their being murdered at an age of complete innocence of personal sin would appear to indicate that they have been chosen to become martyrs of Christ.

It seems, therefore, that all aborted children *could* actually be martyrs of Christ. Just as the Holy Innocents of Bethlehem were murdered ultimately because of the hatred of Satan for the seed of Mary, Mother of Jesus and of the Church (Gen 3:15), so also are aborted children murdered ultimately because of the hatred of Satan for the seed of Mary, Mother of Jesus and of the Church, and, therefore, of every woman precisely because such children have the potentiality to know, to love, and to serve God in this life and afterwards to be happy with him forever in Heaven. Aborted children are like the Holy Innocents of Bethlehem, for the dagger of Satan strikes them as potential members of the Mystical Body of Christ – as pre-born children who might soon in this life have Christ living in their hearts. But *would* God ever give to Satan the power by acts of murder to rob unborn children of any chance to receive the saving grace of Christ?

Rachel weeping

Regarding the death of the Holy Innocents of Bethlehem, Matthew 2:18 quotes the prophet Jeremiah as saying: 'A voice was heard in Rama, lamentation and great mourning: Rachel bewailing her children, and she would not be comforted, because they are not' (Jer. 31:15). This voice was literally the lamentation of the Jewish mothers of these infant children. But Jeremiah offered hope to those mothers who awaited the Saviour, for he went on immediately to add: 'Thus says the Lord: Let your voice cease from weeping, and your eyes from tears, for there is a reward for your work, says the Lord: and they shall return out of the land of the enemy' (Jer. 31:16). They will never return on the face of this earth, but they will return in the new creation, for 'the Lord has created a new thing upon the earth: a woman shall encompass a man' (Jer. 31:22). That is, a woman, without receiving male seed, shall engender a man in her womb – a prophecy of the Virginal Conception of Jesus in the womb of Mary.[11] And Jesus will lead them out of the land of the enemy into Heaven.

In the spiritual sense of Jeremiah 31:15, Rachel symbolizes both the Church of Jesus Christ and the Heart of the Blessed Virgin Mary. The questions before us are whether this prophecy of Jeremiah refers also to aborted children and whether the Church in our time is fully observing her role in the second part of the prophecy, which may be to recognize that 'they shall return out of the land of the enemy' as martyrs of Christ.

Baptism of blood and of desire

Since all aborted babies have immortal human souls, we know that the souls of all aborted babies are really existing somewhere. St Thomas Aquinas conjectured that children under the age of reason who die without Baptism will live forever in a place of natural happiness called the Limbo of Children.[12] However, St Thomas was not dealing specifically with the case of innocent victims of murder, such as are aborted children. Nor was he affirming that these children do not receive Baptism of blood or Baptism of desire. He does note, though, in treating of the question of evil, that 'since children before the use of reason do not have an inordinate act of the will, neither will they have one after death'.[13] In his commentary on the *Sentences* of Peter Lombard, St Thomas points out that 'Baptism does not require a movement of free will, because it is administered principally against original sin', and thus can be given to those who do not recognize it'.[14] But he also says a little earlier that he alone can receive Baptism who can 'participate in bodily washing; therefore, not a child resting in the womb of his mother.'[15] Thus St Thomas makes clear that here he is talking only about Baptism of water, for he does not deny that John the Baptist was sanctified in his mother's womb without being so washed.

On the contrary, in his *Catena Aurea*, at Luke 1:41, St Thomas quotes St Ambrose saying that John the Baptist leapt in his mother's womb because 'he felt grace' ('*gratiam sensit*'), and he cites Origen affirming that at this moment 'John was filled with grace that flowed over into his mother.' Similarly, regarding the fate of the Holy Innocents, St Thomas affirms in his Commentary on Matthew (2:18) that the Church either 'considers them to be reigning and so rejoices over them as over reigning persons', or 'awaits [their] consolation in the future'. And, in the *Catena Aurea* at Matthew 2:18, St Thomas quotes St Hilary saying that the Holy Innocents 'were carried away through the glory of martyrdom to the higher status (*profectus*) of eternity', and he cites Rabanus Maurus affirming that 'this means that the Church does weep over the taking away of saints from this world, but she does not want to be consoled in the sense that those who have overcome the world by their death should return to endure again the struggles of this life, because they must not be called back again into this world.'

Writing in his *Summa Theologiae*, St Thomas asks 'whether anyone can be saved without Baptism', and he replies that one can be saved without actually being baptized (with water) if he has a desire to be baptized which comes 'from faith working through charity' (Gal 5:6), 'through which God, whose power is not bound by visible sacraments, sanctifies the man interiorly'.[16] Thus, he says, a catechumen having the desire to be baptized who dies before receiving the sacrament does not arrive immediately at eternal life, but will suffer a penalty for his past sins; he will, however, be saved, 'yet so as by fire' (1 Cor. 3:15).[17] Thomas asserts that, since infants still in the womb cannot be washed with water, they cannot be baptized at all,[18] meaning that they cannot be baptized with water, though he adds that, if the mother should die while an infant was living in her womb, the womb should be opened and the fetus should be baptized.[19] He observes, importantly, that babies in their mothers' wombs 'can nevertheless be subjected to the action of God, in whose presence they are living, in such wise that they achieve sanctification by some privilege of grace, as is evident regarding those who have been sanctified in the womb.'[20]

Newly born babies cannot consciously intend to be baptized, yet they are validly baptized into the Church. St Thomas addresses this problem by affirming that

just as children in their mothers' wombs do not take nourishment by themselves, but are rather sustained from the
nourishment of their mothers, so also children not having the
use of reason are situated as it were in the womb of Mother
Church, and they receive salvation not by themselves but by
an act of the Church ... And for the same reason they can be
said to intend [to receive the sacrament], not by an act of
their own intention, since they sometimes cry and try to resist,
but through the act of those by whom they are presented.[21]

St Thomas quotes St Augustine in response to the objection that
babies do not have faith and sometimes even the parents are
lacking in faith.

In the Church of the Saviour small children believe through
others, just as the sins which are remitted in Baptism have
been received from others ... (Thus) small children are
presented to receive spiritual grace, not so much by those in
whose hands they are carried, although also by them if they
too are true believers, as by the whole society of saints and
faithful.[22]

St Thomas adds:

And the infidelity of their own parents, even if after their
Baptism they try to taint them with sacrifices to demons, does
not harm the children ... But the faith of one [person],
indeed of the whole Church, benefits the little child through
the action of the Holy Spirit, who unites the Church and
communicates the good things of one [individual] to
another.[23]

Hence the fact that unborn babies cannot consciously know the
object of faith and express their love for God by an act of their
will does not exclude their sanctification at the moment of their
death through the grace of Jesus made available in his Church,
even though they have done nothing themselves to merit it. St
Thomas points out that in any case no one can merit for himself
the first grace he receives.[24] Thus, from St Paul: 'Not by works of
justice which we have done, but according to his mercy he saved
us, by the laver of regeneration and renovation of the Holy Spirit,
whom he has poured forth upon us abundantly through Jesus
Christ our Saviour: that, being justified by his grace, we may be

heirs according to hope of life everlasting' (Titus 3:5–7). But, continues St Thomas, one human person can obtain for another the grace of sanctification, not by the worthiness of his act but by an acceptable supplication of divine mercy, 'according to the degree of friendship' that the beseeching person has with God.[25] It is evident, moreover, that no man has a closer degree of friendship with Jesus and with every baby being lethally attacked by Satan than has the Blessed Virgin Mary. It follows that Mary can merit by her prayers the grace of Baptism for these infants. As Mary, at the foot of the Cross, joined in the self-offering of her Son Jesus for the redemption of all mankind, so can she present to God each unborn infant brought by his earthly mother 'like a sheep to the slaughter', and she can give testimony for each infant as he stands 'as dumb as a lamb before his shearer' (cf. Isa. 53:7) while his body is being stripped away from his soul.

Repentance for abortion

Furthermore, the Church has confirmed the salvation of the Holy Innocents through Baptism of blood and has offered hope that 'there is a way of salvation for children who have died without Baptism' (*CCC*, no. 1261). Supposing that there is a way of salvation for aborted children, it is possible – as already suggested – that they tend to be situated among those who are crying out with a loud voice, saying, 'How long, O Lord, holy and true, do you not revenge our blood on them that dwell on the earth?' (Rev. 6:11). The place of these souls, who were 'slain for the word of God and for the testimony which they held,' is 'under the altar' (Rev. 6:9). They are under the altar of the Cross of Jesus on Calvary. If they are inclined to cry out for revenge against those who dwell on earth, the Church can help to mitigate that desire. The Church can foster acts of repentance on the part of parents who have aborted a child, on the part of those who have participated in abortions, and on the part of all others who share the guilt as members of human society. Repentance and reparation can heal the wound of death inflicted upon aborted babies and reestablish the bond of love between child and parent. Martyrs of Christ would want to save their human murderers from the pains of Hell, so as to direct their indignation solely against the evil spirit, Satan, who is their ultimate enemy and who will not repent for all eternity, because he is the permanent enemy of God.

There is an aspect of social responsibility in the crime of abortion. Death came upon all men as a result of the sin of one man, and that is also why infants are conceived in the state of original sin. This somewhat mysterious solidarity of all human beings with one another in the circumstances of human society has its effect in the case of abortions. The example has been brought forward of the murder of a person by an unknown assailant in Deuteronomy 21:1–9. The elders of the nearest town were told by God to sacrifice an unbroken heifer and to wash their hands ceremoniously over the slain heifer and pray to God that this innocent blood not be laid to their charge 'in the midst of thy people Israel,' and then 'the guilt of blood shall be taken from them.' Certainly, in the case of abortion, it is Jesus, the innocent Lamb, who has been sacrificed for human society, and it is the Church, especially through the Mass and the other sacraments, that pleads with God not to hold these murders to general account. But designated prayers and rites for each distinct abortion are still largely lacking. Public prayers are made in Scripture in order to exorcise the sin of idolatry. Just as so often in the past demons have demanded sacrifices of children to themselves, so also in our time the sin of abortion is a kind of sacrifice by parents of their children to demons. And demons are demanding these latter-day sacrifices ultimately because of their hatred for Jesus and his Mother.

Of these stones

John the Baptist called people to a baptism of repentance in preparation for the coming Judgment. Allegorically, John the Baptist typifies repentance in preparation for the coming of the sanctifying grace brought by Jesus. John stood in the River Jordan to administer the baptism of penance and repentance (Matt. 3:6). Etymologically, the name Jordan derives from the Hebrew verb *yārad*, meaning 'to come down', or 'to descend',[26] with an *n* added to make *yā-dēn* in the Masoretic text. But the word was originally *yār-dēn*,[27] that is, 'flowing down from *dan*', which means 'judge' or 'judgment'.[28] In fact, the tribe of Dan occupied the region around the sources of the Jordan and built their city of Dan there (Judg 18:29). Allegorically, then, the Jordan signifies Jesus as the incarnate Word having come down to earth from the heavenly Judge to free mankind from the judgment incurred by the original sin of Adam and Eve, and thus it signifies also the sanctifying grace that flows out from the Heart of Jesus (John 7:37–38) through the

sacraments of the Church, beginning with the sacrament of
Baptism, and the gift of the Holy Spirit (John 7:39; cf. John 1:33).

John the Baptist declared to the Pharisees and the Sadducees
that 'God is able of these stones to raise up children to Abraham'
(Matt 3:9). We are certain that God is able of any stones to raise up
children to Abraham, but we are here reminded of the twelve
stones, carried by representatives of the twelve tribes of Israel, that
Joshua had had placed in the dry bed of the Jordan at the time of
the crossing over into the Promised Land (Josh. 4:9). These stones
signify the Church of the New Testament, rooted in the Death and
Resurrection of Christ, whose members have been made 'the seed
of Abraham, heirs according to the promise' (Gal. 3:29). If Jesus
could convert the hardened heart of an inveterate criminal into a
humble and suppliant seeker of his Kingdom (Luke 23:42–43), he
can convert the dormant hearts of victimized babies into beseech-
ers of his grace and lovers of his holy Face.

> For I will take you from among the Gentiles and will gather
> you together out of all the countries and will bring you into
> your own land. And I will pour upon you clean water, and you
> shall be cleansed from all your filthiness, and I will give you a
> new heart and put a new spirit within you; and I will take away
> the stony heart out of your flesh and will give you a heart of
> flesh. And I will put my spirit in the midst of you, and I will
> cause you to walk in my commandments and to keep my judg-
> ments and to do them. And you shall dwell in the land which
> I gave to your fathers, and you shall be my people, and I will
> be your God (Ezek. 36:24–28).

> O Lord our Lord, how admirable is your name in the whole
> earth! For your magnificence is elevated above the heavens.
> Out of the mouth of infants and of sucklings you have
> perfected praise because of your enemies, that you may
> destroy the enemy and the avenger (Ps 8:2–3).

The transforming love of Jesus is illustrated by his action at the
wedding feast of Cana (John 2:1–11). The need of the newly
married couple is satisfied miraculously by Jesus, not because of
their conscious request, but at the request of Mary. The changing of
water into wine symbolizes allegorically the future changing of wine
into the Blood of Jesus. And it signifies tropologically – in terms,
that is, of its implications for human living – the changing of merely
human needs and aspirations into sanctifying grace and supernat-

ural life. Babies being attacked by the knife or the pill of the abortionist still have for a moment the water of human life, but they do not have the wine of sanctifying grace. It is believed by some that Mary, Mother of the Church, feels this need in her heart and says to Jesus in every case: 'They have no wine'. There is a growing feeling that, even though the usual time may not yet have arrived for the administering of Baptism of water, Jesus works a miracle of grace, out of his own compassionate love for these innocent children, but also because of the request of his Mother.

So far, we have not offered a similarly tropological account of the Gospel references to the Jordan. Tropologically, the Jordan represents the flow of human history down from Adam and Eve, who were judged guilty of original sin and who thus infected the whole of the human race except for Jesus and Mary. Human history can help itself only by way of the baptism of repentance and of acts of penance. But Jesus came and stood in the Jordan, thereby (allegorically) sanctifying its waters in the sacrament of Baptism and in all of the works of sanctifying grace. Jesus submitted at the same time to the baptism of repentance and of penance, not because he in any way needed this himself, but because he came to take the guilt of the whole human race upon his shoulders, and also, as he said, 'for so it is fitting to us to fill up all justice' (Matt. 3:15).

Let us try to apply these notions to the case of aborted children. Their lives in the womb have flowed down like the mystical Jordan river from the judgment upon their first parents. They have been infected with the penalty of original sin, and have had no opportunity to make acts of repentance or to believe in the truth of Christ. But they are not guilty of personal sin. We have been assured that, even if the hearts of these children were as hard as stone, God could raise them up to be children of Abraham and sanctified members of the Church. But *their* hearts have *not* been hardened. Could this violent and unjust death be *their* 'act of repentance'? Could the faith of the Church express their faith for them? We know that, in the water-Baptism of an infant, it is the faith of the sponsors or the faith of the Church that expresses the child's faith. John the Baptist did not receive Baptism of water. He was sanctified in his mother's womb by Jesus, brought near to him by Mary, while a role was also played by the faith of John's mother, who spoke for him (Luke 1:41–45). Now, Mary is the Mother of the Church and the spiritual Mother of everyone born into the Church (John 19:26).[29] Indeed, she is in a real sense the mother of every infant in the womb.[30] May we not hope that Mary brings Jesus to the side of every infant being criminally slaughtered in the womb and that her faith speaks for the infants who cannot speak? The Church, too, is the mother of all the regenerated, and the Church, through its members, has recourse incessantly to Mary to 'pray for us sinners now and at the hour of our death'. Is it conceivable that Mary does not pray for these innocent victims of abortion at the hour of their death with an efficacious prayer that enables their Baptism of blood or of desire? It seems hardly conceivable.

To fill up all justice

However, if these aborted infants have received Baptism of blood, they do not *per se* need to be claimed by the Church in order to be able to enter Heaven. In point of fact, if they have received Baptism, they are already members of the Church. Nevertheless, it seems fitting that the Church on earth should wash these sanctified souls with the tears of those guilty of the crime of abortion 'in order to fill up all justice.' To proclaim aborted children as martyrs would encourage remorse in the hearts of those who have killed them, since the guilty will know that they will have to face these children in the life and the Judgment to come. And the acclaiming of these children would encourage their parents to pray to them for forgiveness, thus bringing hope into the lives of the guilty. Such a recognition would also be a blow against Satan, who cannot bear to see good brought out of evil. In view of this as yet unfulfilled need, it appears that the Church should develop a more detailed and explicit spirituality of repentance, including suitable liturgical rites and celebrations, above all for those who have been directly involved in the sin of abortion, but also for all the members of the Church and of human society as a whole.

Pope John Paul II says to women who have had an abortion:

> Do not give in to discouragement and do not lose hope. Try rather to understand what happened and face it honestly. If you have not already done so, give yourself over with humility and trust to repentance. The Father of mercies is ready to give you his forgiveness and his peace in the sacrament of Reconciliation. You will come to understand that nothing is definitively lost and you will also be able to ask forgiveness from your little child, who is now living in the Lord (*qui nunc in Domino vivit*).[31]

If the souls of aborted babies are 'now living in the Lord', it seems likely that they are members of the Mystical Body of Christ, and therefore that they have received either Baptism of blood or Baptism of desire.

Mary, Mother of the Church

Rachel was the mother only of Joseph and Benjamin among the twelve sons of Jacob, but, as the principal wife of Jacob she represents in Jeremiah 31:15 the motherhood also of Judah, in which tribe Bethlehem lay, and of all the children of Israel. Mary, as the Mother of Jesus and the principal recipient of his grace, has been made Mother of the Church and Mother of all the regenerated in Christ.[32] As a result of original sin, all the descendants of Adam and Eve except Jesus and Mary have been conceived partially subject to Satan (cf Col. 1:13; Heb. 2:14–15), but they do not fully become his 'seed' (Gen. 3:15) unless by their own wilful serious sin. Only Jesus and Mary have been conceived entirely free of subjection to Satan, so it is against them that the seed of Satan especially vent their hatred. The growth of devotion to the Hearts of Jesus and Mary has enabled the Church better to understand the merciful love of Jesus and the role played by Mary in the salvation of the people of God.

> Taken up into heaven [Mary] did not lay aside the saving office but by her manifold intercession continues to bring us the gifts of eternal salvation. By her maternal charity, she cares for the brethren of her Son, who still journey on earth surrounded by dangers and difficulties, until they are led into their blessed home. Therefore, the Blessed Virgin is invoked in the Church under the titles of Advocate, Helper, Benefactress, and Mediatrix (*Lumen Gentium*, no. 62).

Thus in *Lumen Gentium*, the Dogmatic Constitution of the Second Vatican Council on the Church, the Church proclaims Mary to be the Mother of God, the Mother of the Redeemer, and the Mother of the members of Christ (nos. 53 and 61). Conceived without the least stain of original sin (no. 59), she cooperated with the work of salvation (nos. 56 and 61), and she 'faithfully persevered in her union with her Son unto the Cross, where she stood, in keeping with the divine plan, enduring with her only-begotten Son the intensity of his suffering, associating herself with his sacrifice in her mother's heart, and lovingly consenting to the immolation of this victim who was born to her' (no. 58). Thus, 'by reason of the gift and role of her divine motherhood' and 'with her unique graces and functions, the Blessed Virgin is also intimately united to the Church. As St Ambrose taught, the Mother of God is a type of the Church in the order of faith, charity, and perfect union with Christ ... The Son whom she brought forth is he whom God placed as the firstborn among many brethren (Rom 8:29), that is, the faithful, in whose generation and formation she cooperates with a mother's love' (no. 63). The faithful on earth are moved to a filial love towards their mother in Heaven and to the imitation of her virtues (no. 67). 'In the meantime the Mother of Jesus in the glory which she possesses in body and soul in heaven is the image and beginning of the Church as it is to be perfected in the world to come. Likewise she shines forth on earth, until the day of the Lord shall come (cf. 2 Pet. 3:10), a sign of certain hope and comfort to the pilgrim People of God' (no. 68).

We may, therefore, ask ourselves how children at the moment of being assaulted unto death in the wombs of their mothers may appear to the merciful Heart of Jesus and the maternal Heart of the Blessed Virgin Mary: that is, how these babies, who will never be born into this world, may appear to Jesus, who is 'the firstborn among many brethren', and to Mary, who 'cooperates with a mother's love' in the generation and formation of the brethren of Jesus. St Paul writes to the Colossians: 'And you, whereas you were sometime alienated and enemies in mind and in evil works, yet now he has reconciled in the body of his flesh through death, to present you holy and unspotted and blameless before him' (Col. 1:21–22). One can hope that the same grace may be given also to babies, lethally attacked, who have never been enemies of God either in mind or in evil works.

We can compare the fate of these babies with the fate of the Good Thief facing death on his cross. He was at first inclined to join his criminal companion in mocking the crucified Jesus (Mark 15:32), thus adding outrage to Jesus to the other sins that he had committed 'in mind and in evil works'. Yet he was led to repent and to beseech Jesus to remember him when he came into his kingdom, and Jesus took him into that kingdom (Luke 23:42–43). How did this man receive the grace to repent and to ask for Heaven? Undoubtedly, because he was forgiven by the all-merciful Heart of Christ (cf. Ps. 102[103]). But Mary was also standing there. The Gospel does not tell us, but one can surmise that this man was helped as well by Mary's prayers for him and by her presence at the foot of the Cross. He was sanctified without Baptism of water because of a desire for Heaven which she helped him to conceive.

Similarly, in the case of aborted infants, where the wombs of their mothers become the places of their death, it seems altogether likely that Mary comes to stand beside them, carrying in her maternal Heart the merciful love of the sacred Heart of Jesus. If the thief on Calvary could be given the grace of desire for Heaven, so can these infants. They could be given a supernatural enlightenment by Jesus at the painful moment of their death or, if not, then their faith could easily be represented by Mary as their Advocate and Sponsor, as Mother of the Church. In fact, the opposite case appears unthinkable, namely, that Mary, Mother of the Church, does not come to stand beside them and to speak words of faith for them at the agonizing moment of their death. So the issue hangs on the basic desire for life of the infants and the needed help from the Hearts of Jesus and Mary. One's mind travels back to the presentation of Jesus in the Temple and the prophecy of Simeon, who said at that time to Mary: 'Behold this child is set for the fall and for the rise of many in Israel, and for a sign which shall be contradicted. And your own soul a sword shall pierce, that out of many hearts thoughts may be revealed' (Luke 2:34–35). It is a matter of fact that the knife that pierces the heart or the brain of these aborted babies pierces also the Heart of Mary. And thus it follows that, because of this sorrow accepted freely by the Heart of Mary, revealed thoughts, that is, thoughts of faith and love for Jesus, may well come forth at the moment of their death, either directly from the hearts of these unborn babies or vicariously from the Heart of Mary acting as their Mother and their Advocate.

Finally, then, let us return to the thought of 'Rachel weeping for her children' (Jer. 31:15) in the context of Mary's motherhood of the Church and of all those born of women. If Mary is the spiritual Mother of all men and women, then babies assailed by abortion are mystically in her womb. Mary weeps for babies murdered by abortion, but in this she will be comforted, because she knows that Jesus will lead them out of the land of the enemy (Jer. 31:61). But Mary weeps also and more bitterly for those of her children who commit the abortions or favour them in any way, and in this she will be comforted only inasmuch as these sinful people, mothers, fathers, and others, repent and do penance for their sin. By her sorrow and her suffering, Mary helps them to repent. Perhaps this is the meaning of Apocalypse 12:2, as it applies to Mary assumed into Heaven: 'And being with child, she cried travailing in birth, and was in pain to be delivered.'[33] Mary wants to be delivered of the pain that she suffers for these innocent babies, until they have found their place in eternity, and she wants even more to be delivered of the pain that she suffers because of the sins of abortion perpetrated upon them. The Church can offer its devotion to Mary by encouraging prayers and acts of reparation for these sins and by helping to restore the bond of love between these babies and their parents. This may indeed be a message for our time.

Synthesis and conclusion

St Thomas Aquinas postulated the existence of a Limbo of Children as a place of eternal natural happiness for children under the age of reason who died without benefit of the sacrament of Baptism. In our time, the *Catechism of the Catholic Church* gives reason for us 'to hope that there is a way of salvation for children who have died without Baptism.' The case of aborted children is even more hopeful in that they are innocent victims of murder. In proposing a Limbo of Children, St Thomas was not specifically thinking about victims of murder, and the Catholic Church has long recognized the Holy Innocents as martyrs who have received Baptism of blood.

The case of aborted children is clearer today than it was in the time of St Thomas. It is now known and taught with certainty by the Church that the human fetus is a human being from the first moment of fertilization of the ovum.[34] This means that a fertilized human ovum, from the first moment of conception, has a human soul equipped with human intelligence and free will, even though the fetus does not become conscious before a sufficient bodily base has been built up. But the fertilized ovum is already a human being called by God to eternal life with him in Heaven, a being already objectively redeemed by Christ through the Sacrifice of Calvary (cf. *CCC*, no. 1703).

The sacrament of Baptism is intimately tied to the Sacrifice of Jesus on Mount Calvary. All of the grace of the seven sacraments of the New Law flows from the Blood of Jesus poured out from the Cross and from the Sacred Heart of Jesus, wounded for our salvation. Even before the Passion and Death of Jesus, the Holy Innocents were saved by the shedding of their blood without Baptism of water. John the Baptist was sanctified in the womb of his mother, only later to confirm his witness by the supreme sacrifice of his life. At the dawn of history the voice of the just Abel's blood cried out to the Lord God from the earth. There is theological evidence that the voice of the blood of each aborted baby calls out to God from the 'earth' of his earthly mother's womb as well as from the spiritual womb of the Church and from the mystical womb of the Blessed Virgin Mary, Mother of the Church and spiritual Mother of all the descendants of Adam and Eve.

Satan hates all the physical descendants of Eve and all the spiritual children of Mary (Gen. 3:15); he hates all human beings from the moment of their conception, because they have the potentiality to become children of God and heirs of Heaven. In fact, every human fetus or fertilized human ovum is potentially a child of Mary and a member of the Church, and it is for this reason especially that Satan makes war against them (Rev. 12:17). Crimes of abortion are ultimately attacks of Satan against the seed of woman and above all against the spiritual seed of Mary.

Jesus has called 'blessed' those who 'suffer persecution for justice's sake', not because they will receive the reward of unending *natural happiness*, but because 'theirs is *the kingdom of heaven*' (Matt. 5:10). Every procured abortion is performed in an atmosphere of opposition to the Law of God. Every procured abortion is an act of subservience to Satan in his hatred of Jesus and of the Mother of Jesus. Every aborted infant has been persecuted unto death because, in the ultimate analysis, he or she is a potential child of Mary in the Mystical Body of Christ. Thus, every aborted infant has suffered persecution, not only on the ground of natural injustice by the suppression of that infant's right to life, but also on the ground of opposition to the holiness of Christ.

St Thomas points out that a knowledge of the object of faith and a movement of free will are not required for the validity of the sacrament of Baptism. If this is so for Baptism of water, it is also true for Baptism of blood, as is proclaimed indeed by the teaching and the Liturgy of the Church. There is reason to hope that the victims of abortion, without making any conscious act, are at the moment of their death sanctified by the Blood of Jesus through the prayer and intercession of the Church, and in particular of the Heart of Mary. This idea, which lacks the support of an official proclamation of the Church, is supplementary to the possibility of a supernatural enlightenment at the moment of their death, whereby these children would see the object of Christian faith and, strengthened by the actual grace of Jesus and the intercession of Mary, would lovingly embrace God with an act of their will. We have reviewed some evidences in Sacred Scripture for these assumptions and possibilities. God is able to raise up stones to become children of Abraham (Matt. 3:9), and all the more clearly to raise up the hearts of innocent children to become members of the Church (Gal. 3:29). This divine power and intention is clearly expressed in Ezekiel 36 and in Psalms 8 and 102 (103). It is also illustrated in other places in Sacred Scripture, such as at the wedding feast of Cana (John 2). These seems to be no doubt that Mary, Mother of the Church, Mary the New Eve, Mary Queen of Heaven is present at the death of every aborted infant, to pray, to assist this baby soul, to intercede with Jesus, to offer her awareness, her sorrow, and her love in sponsorship of this child. As the archetype of Rachel in Matthew 2:18, Mary's tears are sufficient to attract for the dying fetus the forgiveness of original sin, by the sacrifice of his tiny life, by the prayers of her Heart, and by the strength of her love for God in support of the desire for life in this infant soul. A sword once again pierces her Heart so that revealed thoughts may live in the mind and heart of this outraged child (cf. Luke 2:35).

What more can the Church do for aborted children? Like Rachel of old, the Church weeps for the truncated lives of these tiny human persons, but with the hope that Jesus will lead them 'out of the land of the enemy' (Jer. 31:16). Like Rachel of old, the Church also weeps for the murderers of these children, above all for their parents, knowing that these persons will never be led out of the land of Satan, the enemy, if they do not sincerely repent and perform acts of penitence. Both of these reasons seem to call for further initiatives on the part of the Church.

From the evidence presented, it seems to me that aborted souls do not absolutely need to be claimed by the Church in order to be saved or to enter into the eternal happiness of Heaven, if they have already been claimed by Mary, image and model of the Church, Mother of the Church and Mother of all the faithful. Apart from being the spiritual Mother of all mankind as the New Eve, Mary is the Mother of all the members of Christ, 'since she has by her charity joined in bringing about the birth of believers in the Church, who are members of its Head' (*Lumen Gentium*, nos. 53–54). Mary's work of charity might well include bringing victims of abortion into the Church. Thus, these babies would be baptized in the Blood of Jesus, not only by the mingling of their own blood, but also by the faith of the Church, pre-contained and epitomized in the faith and charity of Mary, Queen of Heaven.

Aborted souls desire the repentance of their parents and the establishment of a mutual bond of love with them. The Church could help in this need by developing a more detailed and explicit spirituality of repentance for those involved in the sin of abortion and for the members of the Church as a whole, not excluding suitable liturgical rites and celebrations. These slaughtered victims of abortion have not only witnessed to the moral truth, 'Thou shalt not kill', but they have been killed by a dagger that was aimed ultimately by Satan at the Hearts of Jesus and Mary. By declaring, if possible, the fact of this ultimate aim through the proclamation of these innocent babies as martyrs, the Church could repair the outrage to these infant souls, add millions to its recognized membership, give a new motive for restraint to those who would attempt abortion, strike a powerful blow against Satan and his cohorts, and express in a new and endearing way her filial devotion to Mary and her appreciation for the sanctifying influence of Mary in the lives of her members.

It is, however, the sole prerogative of the Pope and of the universal Magisterium to examine the evidence and to determine whether or not aborted babies can be claimed as members of the Church. In the absence of such a determination, the faithful may not presume this, but can only hope and pray, reassured that in the end, whichever be the case, 'God shall wipe away all tears from their eyes: and death shall be no more, nor mourning, nor crying, nor sorrow shall be any more, for the former things are passed away' (Rev. 21:4).

Notes

1   Thus, for example, Patricia de Menezes in a personal letter to this writer, dated 15 June 1995. Her opinion is expressed in a series of statements, entitled *Scriptural References and Documentation Relevant to the Proposed Claiming of Aborted Children as Companion Martyr Saints of the First Holy Innocents*, of which I have seen 177 printed pages. The present essay touches upon some elements of this opinion in the context of the general question of the destiny of aborted children.

2   Cf. Congregation for the Doctrine of the Faith, *Donum Vitae*, no. 6.

3   Cf. Pope John Paul II, *Evangelium Vitae*, no. 58.

4   L. L. Morrow, *My Catholic Faith. A Catechism in Pictures* (3rd edition, Kenosha, Wis: My Mission House, 1954) p. 253.

5   D. Attwater ed., *The Catholic Encyclopaedic Dictionary* (London: Cassell, 1949, 3rd edition), p. 292, 'Limbo', Cf. L. Bouyer, *Dictionary of Theology* (Et New York: Desclée, 1965), p. 276, 'Limbo'. The Latin word *limbus* means a border, edge, or fringe.

6   R. Lawler, D. Wuerl and T. Lawler (eds.), *The Teaching of Christ* (Huntington, Ind: Our Sunday Visitor, 1976), p. 529.

7   Aquinas, *S. Th.*, II–II, q. 124, art. 5.

8   Cf. *Catechism of the Catholic Church*, no. 2853.

9   Cf. Pope John Paul II, *Mulieris Dignitatem*, no. 11.

10   Cf. Pope John Paul II, *Redemptoris Mater*, nos. 23–24.

[11] Cf. C. Lattey in *A Catholic Commentary on Holy Scripture* (London: Thomas Nelson and Sons, 1953), p. 584. The Hebrew verb *sābab* means basically 'to turn around', 'to go around', or 'to surround' (see F. Brown, S. R. Driver, C. A. Briggs, *Hebrew and English Lexicon of the Old Testament* (Oxford: Oxford University Press, 1907), p. 685. In the Poel form (used in Jer. 31:22) it always means 'to go around' or 'to encompass' (see p. 865), although with the connected purpose of protecting (cf, e.g., Ps. 26:5[6]). The *RSV* rendering, 'a woman protects a man', thus appears to be an evasion of the literal meaning and a contradiction to the context, since a woman protecting a man is not 'a new thing' created on the earth. Similarly, the rendering in the *Jerusalem Bible*, 'the Woman sets out to find her Husband again', exchanges the literal meaning of the words for a creative interpretation of the translators. Guy Couturier, in the *New Jerome Biblical Commentary* (London: Geoffrey Chapman, 1991), p. 289, suggests the translation 'will protect', as in Deut. 32:10 and in Ps. 31(32):7, 10; however, in all three of these places the verb means literally 'to encompass' (cf the Vulgate, the Douay-Rheims translation, and G. V. Wigram, *The Englishman's Hebrew and Chaldee Concordance of the Old Testament* [London: Samuel Bagster & Sons, 1880, 4th edition], p. 865).

[12] Aquinas, *De Malo*, q. 5, art. 2 and 3; *In IV Sent.*, bk. 11, dist. 23, q. 2, art. 2, and dist. 45, q. 1, art. 2.

[13] Aquinas, *De Malo*, q. 5, art. 3, corp.

[14] *In IV Sent.*, bk. 11, dist 23, q. 2, art. 2c.

[15] Aquinas, *In IV Sent.*, bk. 11, dist 23, q. 2, art. 2c corp.

[16] Aquinas, *S. Th.*, III, q. 68, art. 2, corp.

[17] Aquinas, *S. Th.*, III, q. 68, art. 2, ad 2.

[18] Aquinas, *S. Th.*, III, q. 68, art. 11, corp.

[19] Aquinas, *S. Th.*, III, q. 68, art. 11, ad 3.

[20] Aquinas, *S. Th.*, III, q. 68, art. 11, ad 2.

[21] Aquinas, *S. Th.*, III, q. 68, art. 9, ad 1.

[22] Augustine, *Contra duas epistolas Pelagii*, bk 1, ch. 22.

[23] Aquinas, *S. Th.*, III, q. 68, art. 9, and 2.

[24] Aquinas, *S. Th.*, I–II, q. 114, art. 5, corp.

[25] Aquinas, *S. Th.*, I–II, q. 114, art. 6, corp.

[26] Cf. Brown, Driver, and Briggs, *Hebrew and English Lexicon of the Old Testament*, op. cit., p. 432.

[27] Ibid., p. 434.

[28] Cf. Ibid, p. 192.

[29] 'Wherefore this sacred synod, while expounding the doctrine on the Church, in which the divine Redeemer brings about our salvation, intends to set forth painstakingly both the role of the Blessed Virgin Mary in the mystery of the Incarnate Word and the Mystical Body and the duties of the redeemed towards the Mother of God, who is mother of Christ and mother of men, and most of all those who believe (*matrem Christi et matrem hominum, maxime fidelium*) ...' *Lumen Gentium*, no. 54.

30   'The Mother of Christ, who stands at the very centre of (the Paschal)
     mystery – a mystery which embraces each individual and all humanity
     – is given as mother to every single individual and all mankind' (Pope
     John Paul II, *Redemptoris Mater*, p. 23).
31   Pope John Paul II, *Evangelium Vitae*, no. 99.
32   Cf. *Lumen Gentium*, no. 61.
33   Cf. Pope John Paul II, *Mulieris Dignitatem*, no. 30.
34   Cf. Pope John Paul II, *Evangelium Vitae*, no. 58.

3

King Herod and the Martyr-Children

Peter Kwasniewski
International Theological Institute, Gaming, Austria

'God our Saviour ... desires all men to be saved and to come to the knowledge of the truth' (I Tim. 2:3–4). Due to the violent intervention of doctors who 'terminate pregnancies', millions of unborn human beings, long before they could ever 'come to the knowledge of the truth', are heartlessly sent back to the God of love who sent them as gifts to the world. Will not Jesus pour his guiltless blood upon these children in response to the outpouring of their own blood, guiltlessly shed – can he not save by an infinite love those whom he redeemed by an infinite pity? Yet more is involved than God's universal salvific will; there is also the sin of Adam which every human person, except the Mother of God, inherits from the first moment of existence. As a result of the fall man lost the favour with God necessary for communion with him; infected by the sin of his First Parents, he cannot inherit the kingdom of Heaven.[1] Revelation teaches that the only way fallen man can be reunited with God is through the grace of Christ, and that, under the new covenant, this regenerative grace is communicated through Baptism (John 3:5) – primarily the sacrament of Baptism, but also *desire* for this sacrament as well as martyrdom in which the martyr's blood is accepted by God as equivalent to Baptism.[2] Apart from these three modes of Baptism, we know of no other means of salvation.[3] Is there nevertheless a way in which these victims, who are neither regenerated by the waters of Baptism nor old enough to choose to embrace the faith or freely witness to it, can attain salvation? There is one possibility: that infants murdered in the womb suffer a true martyrdom like that of the Holy Innocents, thereby participating in the sufferings and the redemption of Christ.[4] The answer I shall present in this paper is therefore placed expressly in the context of martyrdom or Baptism of blood.

I. Herodian autonomy and the grounds of abortion

The evident *fact* of the massive and systematic persecution of the unborn leads to a fundamental question: 'Why in the world would anyone ever think of killing an unborn child?' We are forced to plunge into the murky depths to discover the act's intrinsic character, its inner structure; we begin to understand how, or to what, the unborn child bears witness, and why this witness is offensive to fallen man. To see how the Holy Innocents of Bethlehem can be the soteriological paradigm for aborted infants, let us focus on the nature of Herod's murderous decree and the way in which the Innocents suffered *for Christ*. I will show, first, that the persecution of the unborn results from a hatred of God, of human nature as the *imago Dei*, and of Christ who has a special love and welcome for all 'little ones' – children, the elderly, the poor, the handicapped, the helpless, the oppressed; and secondly, that this persecution is directed against the unborn precisely as witnesses to natural and supernatural truth.

Herod 'the Great', as he was called by some of his contemporaries, slaughtered the children of Christ's age because he did not want to submit to the reign of Christ the King. He did not want anyone else to rule over him; he wanted only to rule himself – and, of course, to rule others.[5] The Roman Emperors who persecuted Christianity in its infancy stand in league with Herod: the Emperors sought to extinguish a religion that taught the supremacy of another king, another ruler, to whom all earthly knees must bend.[6] If Christianity had *not* exacted this otherworldly allegiance, the Emperors would have left it quite alone. Any bizarre mystery cult or intellectual religion was palatable to the cosmopolitan taste of the Romans; as long as the citizens would tip a spoonful of incense into the fire to honour the divinity of the Emperor who commanded all earthly obedience, then they could go about worshipping or not worshipping whatever god they pleased. But when Christianity came, it declared that there was a higher kingship, a higher *imperium*: 'You would have no power over me unless it had been given to you from above' (John 19:11). To this higher authority all earthly kings and kingdoms must pay homage. As if such a claim were not audacious enough, Christianity went further. It taught that all men who share in the mystery of Christ are adopted sons with him, co-heirs of the kingdom of Heaven – and as a consequence, that all men, from Emperor to slave, are fundamentally equal in the eyes of God.[7] Thus, while in the worldly order the slave negates himself before his master and the citizen falls before his Emperor, in the divine order inaugurated by Christ, the master serves his slave and the Emperor his citizens.[8] All must serve one another in humility and love. The most basic Christian identity is that of servanthood: Jesus tells his disciples that they are to distinguish themselves not as masters but as servants.[9]

At this late time in the history of the West, when Christianity has become so story-book familiar that its radical message is rarely even preached, can we begin to imagine how offensive this religion must have been to the pagans of ancient empires? We must renew in our minds the impression the Christian faith produced: it was a stumbling block, impious and rebellious. Indeed, it was something that had to be not only rejected but *crushed*, for it turned upside-down almost everything that fallen mankind takes for granted. In overthrowing the idols of paganism, Christ did more than introduce the worship of the true God; he destroyed an entire world, an entire philosophy of life, based upon the idolatry of power and self-will. When we venerate martyrs, we venerate those who will not tip a spoonful of incense to the gods of this world; we honour those who by their example, by the offering of their life, prove to a world comfortably entangled in self-love that man is meant to live unto God alone and sacrifice all that he is in the service of others.

A man and woman who conceive a child are bound by natural and divine law to nurture and educate that child, or to give it up for adoption when they cannot take responsibility for its upbringing. They are bound to submit to the demands laid upon them by their children, just as Joseph and Mary devoted their lives to serving the Christchild, and as all faithful parents do when they sacrifice years to the rearing of their children.[10] The child is like a king in that he must be *served*, but he is absolutely helpless, he is all neediness and dependence, he cannot even survive unless cared for by others. He begs to be welcomed; he needs and demands *love*. If there is one person whom all should love, it is the child, the infant, who is pure dependency and trust. Where is the human being who cannot find room in his heart to do this much?

Herod was such a man. Just as there was no empty room in the inn of Bethlehem, there was no receptive room in his heart for another person to take precedence. All that Herod knew is that this promised child would threaten his lovable self, his selfish self-rule; and that was enough of a motive for him to send the soldiers on their horrible mission. In a mockery of his own rulership, Herod slaughtered the most innocent of his subjects, simply to ensure that none of them would grow up to manhood and ask of him some sacrifice of honour, freedom, or power.[11] The ultimate cause of abortion is that some people do not want to have another person 'reigning' over them, another life making claims upon them, absorbing their time and their energy – in a word, making them servants. Whether it be father or mother, relative, doctor, nurse, counsellor, politician, employer, or any other who is primarily responsible for the decision to abort or the collective pressures which bring it about, abortion *objectively* means: I, the adult with power over life and death, will have no ruler but myself alone; I will not serve, I will not show mercy. This child is a nuisance, an inconvenience, a hardship, it will change the way we have to live our lives, and that, finally, is what we cannot allow.

The children abandoned by their parents and murdered by the abortionist are rejected, just as the infant boys were rejected, on account of Christ whom they represent. The Holy Innocents shed their blood in witness to Christ 'who came to *his own* and his own received him not' (John 1:11).[12] They did not meet their death freely confessing a Saviour whom they *knew*, they played no active part in their own martyrdom. They were slaughtered for the same reason Christ was ultimately crucified: self-will, self-rule.[13] As the chief priests, the people, and Pilate rejected Christ in the end, so Herod rejected him in the beginning.[14] In line with two kinds of persecutions, there are going to be two kinds of martyrs: those who are killed on account of professing a Gospel which their persecutors hate, and those, like John the Baptist, who are killed because their presence prevents someone else from living as he or she pleases. The latter kind of martyr, though not giving an explicitly Christian witness, is by no means unrelated to Christ. As victims of the insidious pride which has the kingdom of God as its formal object, their witness to the Messiah is not personal but, so to speak, cosmological. The Holy Innocents died a death of rejection by the world and its powers long before Christ died on the Cross, despised and rejected; they were killed out of the same hatred for God and for his law that will later propel the enemies of Christ and all who have persecuted Christians throughout history.

The witness given by a martyr is brought about or made possible by persecutors who torture or kill him precisely *because* he represents the Creator and the Redeemer to an ungrateful and sinful world.[15] The chooser or provider of abortion murders a human being who bears ontological witness both to the Father's faultless work of creation and to the self-emptying humiliation of the Messiah who came in the form of helpless poverty, unrecognizable littleness. Aborted infants, then, are true martyrs in so far as their death has been chosen with *essentially* the same rejection of God

the Creator and Christ the Redeemer that Herod displayed. They
are martyrs because they bear ontological witness to natural and
supernatural truth – to the creative Lordship of Christ and to the
Gospel of Life. The parallel between the objective reason the
infants of Bethlehem were killed and the objective reason that an
infant is aborted establishes that the victims of abortion are truly
brothers and sisters of the Innocents. It does not matter if parents,
gynaecologists, counsellors, legislators, etc. are unaware of the
object of their hatred, or unaware that there *is* a hatred propelling
them; for there is no question about the *objective* nature of their act,
even if subjectively they may be confused or ignorant.

II. The Child Martyr as *Imago Dei* and *Imago Christi*

Let us consider more carefully why abortion is an act *contra Deum*,
an instance of *odium Dei et Christi*. Of all the infinite ways the divine
nature may be imitated (all the *possibilia* which the divine mind
contains as ideas), God wills certain unrepeatable individuals, of
whom there are not only ideas but *exemplars*.[16] Each creature is
conformed to its own exemplar, its principle of likeness to God, in
this way bearing a unique resemblance to him that is all the more
definite and exalted as we ascend the hierarchy of being. It is not
enough that he *know* the creature, he must *love* it; it is his love, the
act of his gracious will, that brings a possible being into actual existence.[17] Furthermore, although God wills all things on account of
the divine goodness and with an ordering to him as their final
cause, the person, as an intellectual being capable of knowing and
loving him in return, is the only being which God in a certain sense
wills for its own sake.

When we consider the manner in which God and human beings
cooperate in the procreation of new life, we see that parents are
the proximate cause of human nature coming to be in *this* matter,
while God causes the *being* of the composite so generated, as well
as its peculiar form, the rational soul.[18] Certainly, the child, no less
than the parent, only exists because God *wills* this existence; yet
God allows human parents the power to *command*, as it were, an act
of being from him. In the words of von Balthasar:

> Man and woman, created by God according to his image, are to
> be fruitful. But will they bring forth 'images of God'? Will they
> bring forth beings who (according to the second account) are
> in such a close relation to God that he himself will breathe life

into them? Here, once again, human fruitfulness is separated from exclusively worldly fruitfulness by a deep abyss. Purely worldly beings reproduce their entire nature in new members of the species. What does man reproduce? It would be naïve to say that human parents care for the child's body while God looks after the 'soul'; indeed, it would suggest that the human generative power were far below that of animals. Nor is it enough to say, with Fichte, that the 'union of two freedoms' is required in order to bring forth one new human freedom; every case of rape contradicts this. Rather, we should speak of human generative power, in its natural operation, extending into the divine creative power, which opens up and makes itself available in the creation of man. From God's point of view, this constitutes a 'humiliation' of God that is inherent in the most fundamental act of creation; thus he hands over his creatorship, making it dependent on events initiated at the will of creatures. The real depth of this mystery only emerges when the child is seen no longer as '*res patris*' but as a personality in direct relationship with God: in Christianity.[19]

Thus parents have to answer for their offspring: 'What have you done with *this* talent, this individual person you generated by my power?'[20]. The murder of an innocent child is a crime directed at the very *essence* of God in the most profound way, striking against two incommunicable prerogatives of the Creator: the gratuitous gift of being (*esse*), and the creation of intelligent life, the being of a new person or rational creature.[21] To kill a newly-formed child is to commit sacrilege against the divine love which is the source of all creation, to deny by an act of rebellion that which God affirms in all its participated goodness, beauty, and truth. Whoever rejects the newly-conceived person rejects the *imago Dei* in its most elemental simplicity – and to reject the *imago* is to reject the *Deus qui fecit imaginem*, the 'God who made the image'. Bearing in mind that responsibility for the act is distributed, often quite unevenly, among all who are involved, we must see that the crime of abortion, objectively speaking, can stem only from a conscious or unconscious hatred for the providential love and eternal wisdom that bring each and every child into being. Those who kill the unborn child make it a martyr of divine love and wisdom – that is, a person who, by dying a violent and untimely death in the womb, announces all the more clearly, in the face of the world's hatred, the primacy of the 'good news of life' in the natural order, the *evangelium vitae* which prepares the way for the *evangelium Christi*.[22]

Moreover, since Christ is the Word through whom man is created *ad imaginem Dei* (that is, Christ as the perfect image of the Father is he through whom the divine image in man comes to be present), to kill a child in whom the natural image is least defiled is to crucify the innocent Christ anew. It is to reject the mystery of the Incarnation and the gift of salvation *per Crucem*, to reject both the creative Word and his life-giving death on the Cross. The Catholic believer 'who confesses that the Son of God became man at the moment of his virginal conception, has the greatest of all possible grounds for reverence' towards human life from the moment of conception. 'Unborn life has been assumed and therefore divinized by the consubstantial Word. To attack the unborn is to declare war against God ... If the womb has for nine months been found worthy of the presence of God, then the attack on the unborn is an act of sacrilege, the abomination of desolation.'[23] In the unborn child there is a particular likeness to the *kenosis* of Christ in his self-emptying mission of redemption, which begins by taking on human nature in his mother's womb, which his presence hallows. Through Christ, writes St Irenaeus, 'everything is under the influence of the redemptive economy, and the Son of God ... has traced the sign of the cross on everything,'[24] especially on those things that most imitate the condescension and suffering of the Lord. Christ dies in every human being slain out of hatred for his name or his kingship, as Paulinus of Nola teaches:

> It is always he, as in the past so in the present, who bears our afflictions and carries our griefs; it is always he, the Man covered with wounds for us ... He, I say, at this very moment, for us and in us, endures the malice of the world, that endurance may have the victory and power be made perfect in infirmity. He, in you, suffers contumely, and it is *he in you* who is hated by the world.[25]

All hatred against man is directed ultimately against Christ, who is the perfect Man, the principle of mankind, its unity, its ruler – not only because *omnia per ipsum facta sunt*, 'all things were made by him', but even more because he is the *redemptor hominis*: 'the Redeemer of man'. All hatred against children in particular is directed against Christ, for by his own admission, the child is closer in spirit to the kingdom of God.[26] It is not merely the helplessness of the baby but, even more, the horror of the violence done to it that draws down the mercy of our Lord; this violence is being done *to him*, insofar as every sin committed against a member of the human race is committed against the Redeemer and creative Word. 'If Christ is truly the Head of all men, united through His Incarnation to every man conceived, then he truly suffers in every act of abortion, just as he is neglected in the unfed hungry and the naked man without clothes (cf. Matt. 25:42ff.).'[27] Because the aborted infant is a child of the Father and a potential brother or sister of Christ, its murder is a supreme insult to the Lordship of Christ and the Fatherhood of God. The Father sees Jesus and Jesus sees himself in the murdered child, whom the sinfulness of man has rejected in contempt of the most holy instincts implanted in the human heart.[28]

King Herod sought to kill the coming Messiah. 'Impelled to crime, prone to sins which cry for expiation, ready for atrocity, he disregarded the proofs of innocence, abrogated right, confused the lawful with the abominable.'[29] In our times the self-styled rulers of the earth, whether presidents or prime ministers, gynaecologists and 'population experts' or the democratic masses, allow and procure the killing of unborn children created *ad imaginem Dei* in the bosom of the Eternal Word, children whom Christ befriended in his holy Childhood and redeemed with his Blood on Calvary – the Blood of an innocent man spilled to save the Holy Innocents from their inherited sin. By its suffering and death in union with the Holy Innocents who died 'in place of' Christ, the aborted child is accounted a martyr for God its Creator and Christ its Redeemer, its death being the very moment wherein the child becomes 'subject to the action of God ... so as to receive the grace of sanctification' unto everlasting life.[30] Violently deprived of an earthly home and capable of no personal motion towards God, the aborted child receives a heavenly home by the love of Christ for those who are most helpless, in order that its death, which has the Passion of Christ as its ultimate formal object, may serve a redemptive purpose in the economy of Providence, as did the suffering of the Holy Innocents.[31]

III. Ontological conformity to Christ Crucified – the death of Pelagius

According to St Thomas, there are three kinds of Baptism: of water, of blood, and of the spirit.[32] Sacramental Baptism derives its efficacy from Christ's Passion (to which it conforms the baptized person) and from the Holy Spirit as the first cause. Because the power of the first cause surpasses the effect, an unbaptized person may receive the sanctification of Baptism in two non-sacramental ways: 'from Christ's passion, in so far as he is conformed to Christ by suffering for Him,' and 'by the power of the Holy Spirit ... forasmuch as his heart is moved by the Holy Spirit to believe in and love God and to repent of his sins.'[33] According to Thomas, Baptism of blood has a certain superiority over the others, for the two causes which give efficacy to sacramental Baptism – Christ's Passion and the Holy Spirit – act most excellently in it. 'Christ's Passion acts in the Baptism of water by way of a figurative representation; in the Baptism of the spirit or of repentance, by way of desire; but in the Baptism of blood, by way of imitating the divine act itself.'[34] Following Augustine and other Fathers, Thomas defends Baptism of desire and of blood for adults because they have the free will to commit themselves to Christ. If their lives are cut off prior to Baptism with water, their faith, expressed in desire or in the shedding of blood, suffices for the granting of regeneration.[35] Behind this teaching lies the conviction that some kind of faith directed to Christ is necessary for salvation – whether simply an act of faith like that found in Abel or Abraham, a sign of faith as was circumcision among the Hebrews, or a sacrament of faith, Baptism with water.[16] Without a personal or vicarious act of faith, salvation is impossible.[37] Moreover, the 'shedding of blood is not in the nature of a baptism if it be without charity.'[38] This seems to rule out the possibility of a Baptism of blood when death is not accompanied by active faith and charity. Because infants cannot exercise the faculty of choice, Thomas thinks it impossible for them to be saved otherwise than by sacramental Baptism.[39]

Although on the face of it, Thomas's position precludes the possibility of a public recognition of aborted infants as martyrs and therefore as powerful intercessors for a world enmeshed in the culture of death, nevertheless our thesis can be seen as an extension of Thomas's own thoughts on the Innocents of Bethlehem.[40] An objector having remarked that martyrdom 'is sometimes not voluntary, as in the case of the Innocents who were slain for Christ's sake, and of whom Hilary says that "they attained the ripe age of eternity through the glory of martyrdom,"' Thomas replies that they are rightly considered martyrs simply from the fact that 'they were slain for Christ's sake', 'enduring in their own bodies the suffering Christ was to endure', in this way acquiring the martyr's palm 'by the merit of Christ's martyrdom'.[41] In a question concerning the martyr's aureole, an objector plays again upon the lack of free-will in the slain children, since all merit, of which the aureole is a sign, proceeds from free will, and 'martyrdom consists not only in suffering death externally, but also in the interior act of the will.'[42] Recalling that some authors consider the Innocents 'martyrs in act only and not in will', Thomas comments: 'as the Innocents, even though they do not fulfill all the conditions of martyrdom, yet are martyrs in a sense, in that they died for Christ, so too they have the aureole, not in all its perfection, but by a kind of participation, in so far as they rejoice in having been slain in Christ's service'[43] – a service of which they had no knowledge and to which they gave no free assent. They died in the service of the Lord simply by dying *in his place*, as his 'images', giving their lives to satisfy the hatred directed primarily against Christ; and they rejoice eternally in heaven knowing now in full that their barely-begun lives were sacrificed for a cause greater than anything their feeble minds could have glimpsed or their non-existent personal merits could have won. 'Christ did not contemn His soldiers; He promoted them', writes Chrysologus. 'He enabled them to triumph before living. He caused them to gain a victory before fighting. He gave them their crowns before their bodily members. He willed that they should ... possesses heaven sooner than earth, and not become enmeshed in human affairs before possessing the divine benefits.'[44]

Seeing the death of his beloved Son, despised and rejected among men, in the ignominious death of the Innocents and their aborted companions throughout the ages, the Father responds by allowing those who imitate or mystically participate in the Passion of his Son to receive the fruits of his victory over death, in this way revealing the uttermost depths of his compassion. The one who suffers may not know that he is being killed out of hatred for God, but the Lord of life and death knows, and sees in this unchosen suffering a participation in the one absolutely *chosen* suffering of 'the Lamb slain from the foundation of the world' (Rev. 13:8; John 10:18).[45] The iconic assimilation of the child to the crucified Lord is already the *symbol* of charity, a *seed* of charity planted by God. The granting of salvation to the murdered child who has made no motions *ex parte eius* represents the love of Christ on the Cross most perfectly by magnifying and glorifying the gratuitousness of divine love, which does not need the creature to act first. Against Pelagianism in all its forms, our faith has taught from the beginning that the salvation of *any* man – catechumen or martyr, Christian or non-believer – has its origin, its sustenance, and its consummation in the free gift of grace. Seen from this vantage, the salvation of the aborted unborn is the very model of the prodigality and freedom of God's love; for here, there can be no way of falling into a semi-Pelagian compromise, according to which salvation is co-authored by God and man, working together as a team. Even if a person having the use of reason must freely participate in the life of grace in order to merit salvation, the absolutely first and sustaining cause of this participation is God, whose absolute primacy in granting gifts is most evident in the gift of martyrdom, as Chrysologus reminds us: 'At this point, let the hearer consider and notice carefully, that he may know that martyrdom cannot be bought by merit, but comes through grace. In the case of the infants, where nature itself was still held captive, what will-power was present, or what act of decision? Therefore, in the case of martyrdom, we owe it all to God, and nothing to ourselves.'[46] Washed in the Blood of the Lamb, filling heaven with their cherubic voices of praise, these countless children who have no other benefactor than God supremely glorify his mercy and intercede for the merciless on earth.

Can we say, then, what is the Father's ultimate motive, if we may so express it, for receiving the rejected child back into his bosom? Without doubt, he loves the child created to his image; his goodness is the sole cause by and for which the child was brought into being. What is more, the restoration and salvation of the defiled image is the reason his only-begotten Son willed to suffer death on the cross, enabling mankind to be cleansed in the blood of the Lamb and sanctified from within by the working of the Holy Spirit. Yet standing beneath and, as it were, ever nourishing the acts of creation, redemption, and sanctification, is the most fundamental act of God towards the world: *mercy.* St Thomas teaches that divine mercy stands at the foundation of the entire order of creation and providence; that mercy is the fullness of justice and the principle in which justice towards creatures is rooted.[47] Abortion is an 'abomination of desolation' (Matt. 24:15; Mark 13:14), but divine mercy will not be outdone by man's evil. 'Where sin increased, grace abounded all the more' (Rom. 5:20). If there is one supreme lesson our Lord taught to Saint Faustina Kowalska, it is this: there are no limits to the merciful love which burns in his Sacred Heart, the *fornax ardens caritatis:* the 'burning furnace of charity'.

In light of the foregoing analysis, it appears that the Church would have sufficient grounds for a solemn definition of the martyr-status of the victims of abortion – in other words, that she may define, although it would represent a significant doctrinal development, their present enjoyment of heavenly beatitude and their intercessory power. Moreover, one of the most effective steps the Church could take is the establishment of two universal feastdays: Mercy Sunday on the first Sunday after Easter, to teach about and promote devotion to the mercy of God in the Sacred Heart of Jesus, in addition to a Commemoration of Murdered Infants (or Slain Children) on November 3, patterned after the Feast of All Souls and dedicated to praying for the conversion of the persecutors of unborn life and for the transformation of the culture of death into a culture of life. In this way, countless Masses throughout the world would converge in one fervent petition before the throne of God, and the People of God would be ever reminded of the children's plight. In these various ways, the Church – if she chose to refrain from, or felt that she was not authorized to make, any public declaration about the otherworldly status of the unborn – could accelerate the salvation of the infants, assist the overthrow of the abortion culture, and spread the Gospel of Life to every corner of the world.

Notes

1 Instead of underestimating the gravity of original sin as many modern theologians have done, we would do better to agree with St Thomas that Christ came principally to take away *this* sin from mankind, and only after that, to take away actual sins: see III.1.4. (Unless otherwise noted, all citations of Thomas are from the *Summa Theologiae*.)

2 See III, q. 68, art. 2 ad 2.

3 See III, q. 68, art. 1c. The only punishment that could be appropriate to an unbaptized child who has not attained the age of reason would have to be linked with his *nature*, not his personal qualities or choices, for he bears original sin not as a *peccatum personalis* but as a *peccatum naturae* (see *De malo*, 4. 1c.; *Contra gentiles*, IV. 50; CCC, nos. 404–405). Because the soul contaminated with original sin is not personally in rebellion against God, this sin can be remitted without contradicting the self-determination of a created will. The necessity of the eradication of original sin cannot be denied; what must be left open are the *means* by which God can do this. According to common teaching, God is not bound by the sacraments he has instituted; he can give grace *outside* of the sacraments as well (III.68.2c: God's 'power is not tied to visible sacraments'; see L. Ott., *Fundamentals of Catholic Dogma*, trans J. Bastible [Rockford, IL: TAN, 1974] p. 242, pp. 340–41, p. 356).

4 Since the new covenant had not yet been instituted, the Innocents were saved as belonging to the new *by means of* the old covenant which foreshadowed it; for in the eternal plan of God, the saints of the old covenant were saved on account of the new covenant which was to be established by Christ. The sanctification of all men at all times and places, from the creation of the world to its consummation, is effected only by participation in the death of Christ, that is, by belonging in

some way to the *new covenant*. If the souls of aborted infants are to be saved, they too must be received into this new covenant as the Holy Innocents were received into it by the mediation of the old. That the Innocents enjoy a special status owing to their circumcision is true, but not relevant to the question being posed in this paper. If among the Innocents there were several non-Jewish boys who were slaughtered in the chaotic rush of soldiers, can one imagine denying martyr status to them? All the boys who were slain bore witness to Christ and in this witness is their glory. Because Jesus Christ, as true God, is outside of time, the infants who are martyred prior to the new covenant, and those who are killed after its establishment, can be taken up by God as related *in the same way* to Christ if, by bearing witness, they are assimilated to his covenantal death but have no possible access to the sacraments.

5 Those who want no one else to rule over them are also the same ones who, in the arbitrariness of their pride, wish to impose their rule upon as many others as possible. The rejection of a transcendent superior who measures all by the same standard of justice leads to radical self-exaltation and the viewing of others as inferior, as measured by the self and its desires. Of the five Herods mentioned in the New Testament – Herod (Mt. 21:1–19), his sons Herod Archelaus (whom Joseph feared, Mt. 2:22–23) and Herod Antipas (who put John the Baptist to death and before whom Christ was mocked: Mk. 6:14–29 and parallels, Lk. 23:6–17), his grandson Herod Agrippa I (whom an Angel struck dead for blasphemy: Acts 12) and great-grandson Herod Agrippa II (before whom Paul pleaded: Acts 26) – Herod the Great (regn. 40–4 BC) was unquestionably the most depraved. He was notorious for continually putting to death his rivals or anyone who proved a personal hindrance, including one of his ten wives, her relatives, and several of his own children (Aristobulus, Alexander, Antipater). Josephus describes him as 'a man of great barbarity towards all men equally and a slave to his passions' (*The Jewish Wars* I, xxi, 13). Hearing that Herod's own son was among those whom he had ordered to be slain in Syria, Augustus is purported to have said: 'It is better to be Herod's swine than his son' (Macrobius, *Saturnalia*, II, 4) – a remark curiously applicable to modern-day advocates of universal animal rights, who are also generally supporters of abortion on demand. (See *Catholic Encyclopedia* [New York: The Encyclopedia Press, 1913], vol. VII, s.v. 'Herod'.)

6 Note that the most intense persecution of Christianity took place when it was still in its historical *infancy*. The Roman attempts to eradicate Christianity parallel, on a world-historical plane, the Herodian attempt to kill the Messiah before he arrived at maturity.

7 See Jn. 1:12–13, Rom. 8:14–23, Eph. 1:5, Gal. 4:4–7, 1 Jn. 3:1, Acts 10:34, Rom. 10:12, Eph. 6:8–9, Col. 3:11.

8 See Philem. 1:15–16, Eph. 6:9, Col. 4:1; the same is already present in Wis. 6:2–10 and Sir. 32:1–3.

9 See Lk. 9:48, Eph. 5:21, Phil. 2:3, Mt. 20:25–27, Mk. 9:34.

10 III, q. 36, art. 2 ad 2: 'Mary and Joseph needed to be instructed concerning Christ's birth before He was born, because it devolved on them to show reverence to the child conceived in the womb, and to serve Him even before He was born.'

11 St Peter Chrysologus: 'Herod's inhuman cruelty has exposed how far jealousy tends to go, and spite leaps, and envy makes its way. While this cruelty was jealously seeking the narrow limits of temporal reign, it strove to block the rise of the eternal King ... In his earthly fury he hunts Him whom he does not believe to be born from heaven. He moves the soldier's camp to the bosoms of mothers, and attacks the citadel of love among their breasts. He tests his steel in those tender breasts, sheds milk before blood, causes the infants to undergo death before experiencing life, brings darkness on those just entering into the light of day.' 'In fear of a successor, he moved against his Creator. He slew the innocent babies, with intent to kill Innocence Himself ... Their tongue has been silent, their eyes have seen nothing, their hands have done nothing. No act has proceeded from them; then, whence do they have any guilt? They who did not yet know how to live got death. The period of their life did not protect them, nor did their age excuse them, nor their silence defend them. With Herod, the mere fact that they were born was their crime' (*Selected Sermons*, trans. G. Ganss [New York: Fathers of the Church, 1953], pp. 254–55; pp. 256–57).

12 'Isaias had foretold that a virgin would bring forth the God of heaven, the King of the earth, the Lord of the regions, the renewer of the world, the slayer of death, the restorer of life, the author of perpetuity. The very occurrence of the Lord's nativity proved how sad this was for worldly men, how frightening to kings ... Fearing a successor, they tried to slay the Saviour of all men. At length, since they could not find Him, they devastated His country, mixed mothers' milk with blood, and beat to death the infants of His own years. They dismembered the companions of His innocence, because they could not find for punishment sharers in any guilt of His. If they did all this after Christ was already born, what would they in their wild fury have done to Him when he was conceived?' (Chrysologus, *Selected Sermons*, op. cit., p. 242).

13 That Christ disappointed Jewish hopes for a Messianic leader who would establish political self-rule takes on deeper significance when considered in relation to fallen man's restless desire for worldly autonomy or autocracy. The kingdom of Christ is not of this world, His rulership is of an entirely different order (Jn. 18:33–38).

14 The sudden friendship that sprung up between Pontius Pilate and Herod Antipas, son of the Herod who ordered the massacre of the Innocents, is not a mere coincidence recorded by Luke (23:12) for the curious reader. Among other things, it demonstrates the ultimate *identity* of the first Herodian rejection of the infant Christ and the final

Roman-Jewish rejection of Christ the man. The end circles around to meet up with the beginning, just as the legal endorsement of abortion logically necessitates the legal endorsement of euthanasia or any 'purification of unwanted social elements'.

[15] To be persecuted is obviously a necessary *condition* for martyrdom, but it is more. If a sleeping Catholic is attacked and killed by a Moslem out of hatred for the Christian faith, the former can be a martyr – not because he consciously bore witness, but because his very identity as a Catholic was the reason for which the other killed him; the motive specified the generic act of *killing* as an act of *persecution*. If, on the other hand, a Moslem judge ordered the death of a Christian because he had committed a serious crime, the Christian would not be a martyr by anyone's definition. The *motive* of the killer thus figures crucially in the definition of any 'passive' or 'unconscious' martyr such as the Holy Innocents.

[16] See I, q. 14 and especially I, q. 15; also I, q. 44 art. 3.

[17] See I, q. 20.

[18] The generator brings it about that *this* form should be in *this* matter, even though it does not cause the matter or the form as such: I, q. 104, art. 1 (see G. Doolan, *Exemplar Causality as Formal Causality in St Thomas Aquinas* [Washington, D. C.: The Catholic University of America, MA Thesis, 1997], 21ff.; 35). God creates each human soul *ex nihilo*: q. 90 arts. 2–3, q. 118, art. 3; *Contra gentiles* II.87; *De potentia* 3.9.

[19] *Theo-Drama* vol. 11: *The Dramatis Personae*, trans. G. Harrison (San Francisco: Ignatius Press, 1990), pp. 371–72.

[20] See I, q. 106, art. 5, corp.: 'since the form of a thing is within the thing, and all the more, as it approaches nearer to the first and universal cause, and because in all things God himself is properly the cause of universal being which is innermost in all things; it follows that in all things God works intimately [*intime operetur*]. For this reason in Holy Scripture the operations of nature are attributed to God as operating in nature, according to Job 10:11: "Thou hast clothed me with skin and flesh: Thou hast put me together with bones and sinews."'

[21] For this reason, to sin against new human life is worse, in a sense, than to sin against grace, since the rational soul is the recipient, and its existence the condition, of grace. Man can only be redeemed if he has first been created; creation, both positively (in its being) and negatively (in its privations), bears witness to the promise of and the need for redemption. It is for this reason that nature deserves to be named from its relations to grace: it is the foundation or substratum of grace, its precursor, image or ikon, foreshadowing.

[22] There is a sacred irony to the act of martyrdom: it bears *living witness* to the transcendent value of divine truth precisely by *dying*, by 'losing' everything, on its account. In suffering death, the child innocent of personal sin bears witness to the *inviolability* of human life, silently

proclaiming the mercy of a God who brings not only life, but salvation and forgiveness, into the empty heart and the desolate womb.

23 J. Saward, *Redeemer in the Womb* (San Francisco: Ignatius Press, 1993), pp. 164–65.

24 Quoted in H. de Lubac, *Catholicism: Christ and the Common Destiny of Man*, trans L. Sheppard and E. Englund (San Francisco: Ignatius Press, 1988), pp. 218.

25 *Letter* 38, n. 3, in De Lubac, *Catholicism*, p. 416, emphasis added.

26 Consider Guardini's commentary on Mt. 18:3: 'The usual attitude of the adult toward the child is one of either friendly or unfriendly disregard all too evident in the forced, playful tone which he feels obliged to assume toward the young one. To this Jesus says: You do not receive the child because it cannot enforce respect. For you it is unimportant. But let me tell you, wherever there is something defenseless, there am I! A divine chivalry protects that which is unable to protect itself and declares: *I* stand behind it! ... *I* take it seriously – seriously enough to give my life for it. What you do to a child you do to me! ... The child is utterly at the mercy of the unscrupulous adult, whom Jesus warns: Beware! Where you see only a weak creature is, in reality, a divine mystery as delicate as it is holy. He who lays impious hands upon it does something so terrible that it would be better for him to have been put out of the way before like a dangerous animal' (*The Lord*, trans E. Briefs [Washington: Regenery, 1982], pp. 309–310).

27 J. Saward, *Redeemer in the Womb*, op. cit., p. 165.

28 'God compels no one to be virtuous' (St John Damascene, *De Fide Orthodoxa*, 2). He will not prevent people from having their children killed, since it is in the capacity of free will to choose this crime. Wherever man fails to do what is required of him, however, there is some provision of providence by which God makes up for the deficiency, so that nothing may be left unfulfilled that should be accomplished in Christ, nothing absent from His 'full stature' (Eph. 4:13). For the unborn child radically abandoned by its parents, there is no other who can act as parent save the heavenly Father; and He, like a wise magistrate or loving adoptive parents, takes the abandoned child and carries its soul back to His bosom, where, in His love and wisdom, it was first conceived. Like their Lord 'who has a name inscribed which no one knows but himself' (Rev. 19:12), the aborted children have a name which none but He who called them into being knows; they never received a name because those who killed them ignored their claim to the fellowship of mankind. Their anonymity reflects the ineffability of the Lord, their speechlessness proclaims His unutterable love, of which the silent body and blood of Christ offered upon the altar is the loudest proclamation.

29 Chrysologus, *Selected Sermons*, op. cit., p. 256.

30 III.68.11 ad 1: 'Children while in the mother's womb have not yet come forth into the world to live among other men: consequently they cannot be subject to the action of man, so as to receive the sacrament,

at the hands of man, unto salvation. They can, however, be subject to
the *action of God*, in whose sight they live, so as, by a kind of privilege,
to receive the grace of sanctification, as was the case with those who
were sanctified in the womb' (see III, q. 27, art. 1 ad 2; *De veritate* 28.3
ad 3). Although this sanctification requires in addition the gift of
conformity to Christ which is the proper effect of baptism (III, q. 68,
art. 1 ad 3), Thomas also holds (III, q. 66, arts. 11–12) that unbaptized
martyrs are justified unto salvation *without* receiving the character
imprinted by sacramental baptism. The principle that one must be
(physically) born in order to be (spiritually) reborn is strictly true of
logical, not chronological, priority. The soul of Mary was created and
sanctified at the same time, though the moment of conception
preceded logically the moment of sanctification. What Christ says to
the puzzled Nicodemus is true in the natural order of things; in order
for a person to receive baptism he must already be out of his mother's
womb. But divine power can sanctify a soul and conform it to Christ at
any moment, even the moment immediately after conception (since
the impartible rational soul is present in its entirety as the actuality of
the fertilized cell, and thus as the *subiectum* of whatever the soul is
capable of receiving). To the objection that abortions are so frequent
as to make it strange to call the sanctification of the victims a 'privilege', it may be replied that divine mercy knows no end of privileges
and can distribute them lavishly. Thomas held that the privilege of
prenatal sanctification was extremely rare (see III, q. 27, art. 1 and
q.27, art. 6, *Compendium Theologiae* I.224), but the very principles of his
theology permit, almost demand, a much wider extension, since we
are dealing here explicitly with 'the action of God' (III, q. 68, art. 11
ad 1) who is all-powerful and all-merciful.

[31] Of the baptized child, Thomas says: 'The faith of one, indeed that of
the whole Church, profits the child through the operation of the Holy
Spirit, who unites the Church together, and communicates the goods
of one member to another' (IIIa q. 68, a. 9 ad 2; see ad 1). The child
killed out of *odium Dei et Christi*, as a person conformed to the image
of crucified Innocence, would have the 'goods of the members',
namely the grace and favour of Christ, communicated to his soul as
well.

[32] III, q. 66, arts. 11–12.

[33] III, q. 66, art. 11c. Thomas points out (ibid. ad 2) that martyrdom and
conversion of heart are called baptisms not because they are properly
sacraments, but because they bring about the same effect.

[34] III, q. 66, art. 12.

[35] III, q. 68, art. 2c.

[36] III, q. 68, art. 1 ad 1.

[37] III, q. 68, art. 2 ad 3.

[38] III, q. 66, art. 12 ad 2.

[39] III, q. 68, art. 3.; see also q. III, art. 73.3.

[40] Thomas, as well as his scholastic predecessors and successors, never

thematically joined these two topics – the Holy Innocents and unbaptized (or even more specifically, as Albertus Magnus discusses [*In* IV *Sent.*, d. 44], aborted) children. The broad scholastic consensus is that infants who are not incorporated into Christ either by circumcision or by sacramental baptism cannot be saved, and must go to a *limbus puerorum*: nor would the medievals have admitted the comparison I am drawing, since for them it is the circumcision of the Innocents which enabled them to profess vicariously their faith in the coming Messiah. If instead of being martyred the same children had died from a plague, they would still have attained salvation in virtue of their share in the covenant; their suffering on account of Christ gained them a further glory, the palm of martyrdom, for which they deserve the public veneration of the Church (I owe this point, and the reference to Albert, to private correspondence with C. Beiting: for more detail, see his 'The idea of Limbo in Thomas Aquinas', *The Thomist* 62 [1998], 217–44). However, here I am drawing out what seems to me to be a true parallel or correspondence between the Innocents and aborted infants.

[41]   II–II, q. 124, art. 1, corpus: 'these babies in being slain obtained by God's grace the glory of martyrdom which others acquire by their own will. For the shedding of one's blood for Christ's sake takes the place of baptism. Wherefore just as in the case of baptized children the merit of Christ is conducive to the acquisition of glory through the baptismal grace, so in those who were slain for Christ's sake the merit of Christ's martyrdom is conducive to the acquisition of the martyr's palm. Hence Augustine says in a sermon on the Epiphany (*De diversis* 66), as though he were addressing them: "A man that does not believe that children are benefited by the baptism of Christ will doubt of your being crowned in suffering for Christ. You were not old enough to believe in Christ's future sufferings, but you had a body wherein you could endure the suffering of Christ Who was to suffer."'

[42]   *Supplement*, 96.6, obj. 3.

[43]   Ibid., ad 12.

[44]   *Selected Sermons*, op. cit., pp. 257–58. One sometimes hears the following argument: 'If there is automatic salvation for such children as these, it means that it is better for them never to have lived than for them to have lived and risked sinning. But is it ever better not to have lived than to have lived?' Speaking absolutely, it is better for a child to live than to die, since it is natural for man to grow, be born, and live. However, the question 'Is it *ever* better not to have lived than to have lived?' can very well be answered *yes* in some instances, as with infants who die after having been baptized and are saved without having lived their life. For such as these, it is better, *per accidens*, never to have lived than to have lived and risked losing heaven. Moreover, there could be no such thing as 'automatic salvation' for the unborn any more than for an adult. There is salvation for one who is incorporated into Christ, e.g., an unbaptized person who dies a martyr's death; and if an

aborted child is a martyr, then it is better, *per accidens*, for this child to
have died, since he gains heaven. Indeed, it is always better – this is
one of the great paradoxes of the Christian faith – for a person's life
to be cut off by martyrdom than for him to continue living. (It is obviously *worse* for the persecutors.) If aborted children are martyrs, then
it follows that they are better off, in the divine scheme of things, than
children who die from natural causes or accidents – just as an adult
who dies because a pile of bricks falls on his head is not as fortunate
or blessed as the one who dies confessing Christ before a furious
heathen emperor. We must take the words of Chrysologus (quoted
later) seriously: martyrdom is a pure *gift*, the supreme gift because by
it man attains the greatest likeness to that salvific death of Christ
which made possible all other spiritual gifts.

[45]   'Blood-baptism operates not merely *ex opere operantis* as does baptism
of desire, but since it is an objective confession of faith it operates also
quasi ex opere operato' (L. Ott, *Fundamentals of Catholic Dogma*, op. cit.,
p. 357).

[46]   *Selected Sermons*, op. cit., pp. 258–59.

[47]   'Now the work of divine justice always presupposes the work of mercy
and is founded thereupon ... So in every work of God, viewed at its
primary source, there appears mercy. In all that follows, the power of
mercy remains, and works indeed with even greater force, as the influence of the first cause is more intense than that of second causes' (I,
q. 21, art. 4, corpus); 'mercy does not destroy justice, but in a sense is
the fullness thereof' (I, q. 21, art. 3 ad 2); 'God's omnipotence is
particularly shown in sparing and having mercy, because in this is it
made manifest that God has supreme power, that He freely forgives
sins ... the effect of divine mercy is the foundation of all the divine
works' (I, q. 25, art. 3 ad 3). See J. Saward, 'Love's Second Name: Saint
Thomas on Mercy', in *The Canadian Catholic Review* 8.3 (March 1990),
87–97.

[*]   The author wishes to express his gratitude to those who read and
critiqued earlier versions of this essay: Clarissa Kwasniewski, Michele
Schumacher, Christopher Beiting, and Gintautas Vaitoska.

4

Can the Church declare 'holy martyrs' little children slain by abortion?

Denis Biju-Duval
Pontifical Lateran University, Rome

There are several important – and perhaps insuperable – objections to the attribution by the Church of the title 'holy martyrs' to little ones killed by procured abortion. On the supposition that these objections may not be decisive, such a declaration could take place only if they had been debated and overcome. Thus, in the case of the institution of the liturgical feast of the Sacred Heart, requested by Christ through the mediation of St Margaret Mary Alacoque, the Church acquiesced only after the theological difficulties were removed. That is why, quite apart from my personal opinion on this matter, I am happy to contribute to this reflection which, whatever its outcome, will be of service to the Church.
The points I shall discuss will be the following:

1. The question of the animation of the embryo.
2. The question of the salvation of babies who die before Baptism.
3. The question of the nature of the title 'martyrs':
   a. in a general fashion
   b. with regard to the mystery of the Holy Innocents.

The animation of the embryo

The most recent authoritative text on the matter is Pope John Paul II's encyclical *Evangelium Vitae*, at paragraph 60. What are its essential points? To begin with, there is an argument of a philosophical kind aiming to prove that a biologically human individual is only thinkable if it has a human soul – a soul which is, in point of fact, spiritual. This would lead to locating the moment of animation more or less at conception. However, the Pope says explicitly that the Magisterium has not formally committed its authority on this point. *The Catechism of the Catholic Church* takes into account this state of the question when it says not that a human being is a person from conception but that such a being *must be recognised as possessing the rights of a person* (no. 2270). On the level of moral discernment, which is where the encyclical operates, the possibility that one is indeed dealing with a human person is enough to justify the strictest condemnation of abortion.

That poses a problem in relation to the declaration which is our concern in this study. Surely, to declare someone a martyr even the strongest probability of their actual existence does not suffice. Certitude on the point is necessary. This is not only a problem of legal forms; it is a concrete question for the prayer of Christians, the prayer of the Church. For example, it would be deeply worrying, indeed mendacious, to encourage a repentant mother to pray to the 'holy' child 'martyr' whom she had aborted if one were not absolutely certain that such a human being really existed. On the part of Church authority, an act engaging infallibility would be required. Or to put the matter the other way round, the said declaration would presume that the Magisterium had definitively committed itself in a way which so far it has not done; namely, on the truly personal and human status of the embryo.

Is such a commitment possible? The question is a delicate one. On the one hand, infallibility extends as far as may be necessary – including in the realm of natural reason – for defending faith and morals, and one would hardly be unjustified in regarding the personally human status of the embryo as an example of that. But what building-blocks are there on which to found such an engagement by the Magisterium? On the issue of the precise moment of animation considerations drawn from natural reason enter a region of vagueness from which perhaps no exit is possible. For one thing, in the first days following fertilisation, we simply do not have the experimental evidence to affirm the existence of a biologically human individual (so long as twinning or fusion is a possibility individuality is not established). For another, the spiritual dimension of the soul escapes all possible human verification. There remain, it might be said, arguments of a theological kind: if the Church has always believed that the moment of the Incarnation coincided with Mary's *fiat*, that presupposes the creation in that very moment of the human soul of Christ. It might be asked, though, up to what point precisely can or must that which is true of Christ be said of any human person whatsoever.

St Thomas wrestles with the problem but does not come to a definite decision, since he is still willing to consult Aristotelean chronology on this subject. Can we go further than he did?

It is clear that from a certain point on (specifically, fourteen days for what concerns the experimental evidence that we are dealing with a biologically human individual), it appears possible to affirm with legitimate certitude that the embryo is a human person. As yet, however, the Church has not formally made that affirmation. If it is not possible to determine with clarity just where the boundaries of the human population lie, could one admit a formulation that leaves open the question of the all-enveloping vagueness of the first days of life? Would not this risk letting it be thought that the Church permits, or considers less grave, abortifacient interventions in that very early period? May it not be to occasion in those mothers, now repentant, who have made use of such devices as 'morning after' pills or RY 486 a devotion towards an offspring of whose very existence there is no assurance?

The salvation of babies who have died without Baptism

We are acquainted with all the historic and theological data pertinent to the problem. What is involved is the difficulty of reconciling on the one hand the universal goal of salvation which Christ has obtained for us, and on the other the necessity of Baptism if someone is to be saved. It is a matter of two indubitable truths, both founded in Scripture as well as in Tradition and the practice of the Church. However, integrating them satisfactorily into a coherent whole is no simple task. The hypothesis of the 'Limbo of Children' belongs with these attempts. The Church has not condemned that hypothesis, no doubt because it honoured the necessity of Baptism. Yet there are various reasons which makes it increasingly hard to sustain.

It denies the universality of God's will to save and the incomparable power of that salvation in relation to the dominion of sin (cf. Rom. 5: 12–21). How would it be possible to claim with St Paul that 'where sin abounded, grace abounded all the more' if millions of children, without any personal fault of their own, have to be excluded from that grace by dint of original sin alone? At the most one would have to say that 'where sin abounded, grace brought partial repair'.

Furthermore, this hypothesis claims to offer to children who have died without Baptism a 'purely natural beatitude' which appears to be a contradiction in terms. For firstly, such beatitude would necessarily be 'supernatural' in regard to its origin, since the children in question, being unable to acquire it for themselves by means proper to them, would be obliged to receive it from above, by way of a gift which their condition did not merit. And then secondly, in his *Summa contra Gentiles*, St Thomas well shows that what a spiritual creature begins to know that it naturally desires to see directly. And the consequence of *that* is that a 'purely natural knowledge of God' would imply, for the children in Limbo, the everlasting frustrated desire to see God – something that could hardly be truly called beatitude, even of a 'purely natural' sort.

At the extreme opposite, we find theological positions for which children who have died without Baptism are saved without further ado. This would be one particular application of the Rahnerian theory of the 'supernatural existential', or again the opinion which would have it that the death of little children, even when unbaptized, conforms them ipso facto to the death of Jesus.[1] Now, far from endorsing the Church's universal practice of emergency Baptism for infants in danger of death, such an opinion destroys its very foundations. It presupposes an under-estimate of the problem of original sin. If such sin were simply the expression of a kind of external divine condemnation of these children, for God to lift that condemnation in the case of the dying would suffice to resolve the matter. But original sin represents the fact that, lacking the benefit of sanctifying grace from the first moment of their existence, the minds and wills of these children are of themselves unsuited for rising to the vision of God.

In the case of adults, the problem can be transcended by appeal to the theology of the 'baptism of desire'. Since grace can act beyond the visible limits of the sacramental organism of the Church, God in Jesus Christ can offer himself, and wants to offer himself, to all human beings ('in a manner known to God alone' the Council tells us). And so someone who under grace's influx desires salvation can obtain the 'Baptism of desire'. The problem of babies is that they would seem to be incapable as yet of making such an act of will. Some commentators have tried to transpose this 'desire' from the children to their parents but theologically that will hardly hold up. No more than with original sin is grace a mere divine declaration of salvation, extrinsic to man. What is at stake is the deep orientation of the mind and will of the subject concerned, and that is why, for no fault of their own, the salvation of an unbaptized human being cannot be obtained without integrating a personal act under the influence of grace.

There are two ways out of this seeming *impasse*. The first would consist in ascribing to very young children, right from their mother's womb, a capacity for freedom that would allow them eventually to obtain the Baptism of desire. Some anthropological data might lead us to take such an hypothesis seriously. Thus for example, might not recent evidence showing that the fetus enjoys a far more elaborate psychic existence than was hitherto believed lead one to include there a certain dimension of freedom? Again, does not what is known of the testimony of people who have had 'near death' experiences allow one to think that, in the moment of death, a fetus might with the help of grace express an authentic desire for God? Let us not forget that, in the case of Christ, the Letter to the Hebrews affirms his human adhesion to the Father from the first moments of the Incarnation. 'When Christ came into the world, he said ... "Lo, I have come to do thy will, O God"' (Heb. 10: 5a, 7a). With grace, can this capacity be extended to every baby from his mother's womb?

The second possibility would be located more directly in the realm of grace (even though the desire for Baptism, let it not be forgotten, would itself be impossible without the aid of grace). The Church has always believed that the baptized who die in infancy are, thanks to their Baptism, saved – which means that, in their case, baptismal grace necessarily becomes the 'light of glory' and moves them irresistibly to the vision of God. Might it be possible that this same 'irresistible' grace is communicated to those who die without having been able to receive Baptism? Systematically to affirm that, as J.-H. Nicolas does, seems out of the question: it would render useless the emergency Baptism the Church has always demanded. But can certain circumstances lead to such a grace, as they did for the Holy Innocents?

If such circumstances exist, must they necessarily involve the explicit hatred of Christ, or can the simple fact of being an innocent victim of unjust violence be a sufficient reason? Some Gospel passages would let us think so. Does not the poor man Lazarus obtain eternal life from the mere fact of the unjust condition in which the egoism of the rich man has kept him (Luke 16: 25)? Are not children and the poor conformed to Christ by the mere fact of their condition (Matt.: 25, 40 and 45)? Pointing in the opposite direction, however, the episode of the ten lepers would seem to force us to draw a distinction between the problem of illness (which represents, actually, all earthly indigence and hurt) and the problem of salvation (Luke: 17, 11–19).

We have deliberately posed these questions without giving them precise replies because in the present state of theological reflection it would be very daring to adopt a firm position. In her teaching, the Church has never committed herself on this terrain. As with the funeral Liturgy, *The Catechism of the Catholic Church* contents itself with recommending children who have died without Baptism to the mercy of God. And when, more widely, it is the salvation of the unbaptized at large that is in question, it is only 'in a manner known to God' that the Second Vatican Council affirms such salvation as offered also to them (*Gaudium et Spes*, no. 2). It is plain that the actual state of Church teaching does not allow one to settle the dispute between the different hypotheses we have mentioned. For instance, let us suppose that infants who die without Baptism do have the possibility of an act of freedom which, if well oriented, would have the value of a baptism of desire. At that moment, precisely because their act is free, nothing could guarantee that it will always be take the form of desire for Baptism. Could it not lead to the refusal of such? In another order of ideas altogether, cannot being the victim of unjust violence also sometimes lead to a refusal to forgive, and thus to be saved?

Evidently, the whole matter is still debatable, and so nothing in the Church's teaching allows us to say that children who are victims of abortion are *necessarily* saved. That is all the plainer now that the passage in the encyclical *Evangelium Vitae* where the Pope invited women who had undergone abortions to receive pardon from their children who are 'henceforth living in the Lord' has been modified in the definitive version published in *Acta Apostolicae Sedis*: it is the latter that is the normative reference (*Evangelium Vitae*, no. 99). To be in a position to affirm the salvation of infant victims of abortion a private revelation would not do; for we would then be faced with such a revelation's supplying the deficiencies in the deposit of faith. It must be possible to draw the theologoumenon in question from public revelation itself (which could indeed happen under the stimulus of a private revelation as was the case with the mystery of the Sacred Heart, mentioned above). The present state of Church teaching, of the theological hypotheses in vigour and even perhaps of what revelation does and does not say, leaves us in a position fairly far removed, in my opinion, from what be necessary for the declaration in question to be made.

The question of the title of 'martyr'

In the original sense of the word, martyrdom consists of confessing

Christ to the point of dying at the hands of those who reject him. Its model is St Stephen. This confession of Christ is understood in a broad sense as the will to remain faithful to him, including on the moral level. Thus, for example, one can speak of the martyrdom of St John the Baptist, linked to his prophetic denunciation of the sin of Herod, or again of the martyrdom of St Maria Goretti, assassinated for having defended her virginity against sinful solicitations. In both these cases, the object that, in the mind of the executioners, invites assault, is not directly Christ. Rather it is by their fidelity to God and his will that these martyrs stake their very lives. It can happen on occasion that someone is murdered through surprise attack without being able to confess Christ to his executioners face to face. He can still be considered a martyr to the extent that he personally put his life at risk through bearing the Christian name and accepting the obligations that name entails. (This was the case with, for instance, the [Cistercian] monks of Tibherine [Algeria].) Since martyrdom includes the explicit choice of risking one's own person for the name of Christ, it cannot be attributed – in the sense just stated – to babies in their mother's womb. At no point are they in a position to posit such an action. Their only fault is to exist and that too they have not elected.

However, reference to the Holy Innocents whom the Church also recognises as martyrs obliges us to admit the existence of a form of martyrdom that does not involve the will of those who undergo it. The Holy Innocents did not die on account of a personal commitment to the name of Christ. They died because, in killing them, Herod hoped to kill Christ. In Herod's eyes, they are guilty because they could be the Christ, the 'King of Israel', and by this title threaten his position of power. Here, there is a sort of anticipation of the mystery of the Cross. The Holy Innocents are to die in the place of the One who was really targeted, with Christ himself waiting to be overtaken, thirty years later, by a hate like enough to that which struck them down. The mystery of the Holy Innocents is intimately connected, therefore, to the question of hatred for Christ. To hate Christ certainly leads to putting out of the way his explicit witnesses (the martyrs in the usual sense of that word), but it also leads to a hatred for human beings in general, to destroying humanity so as to destroy Christ in the human. Such an attempt is feasible because God became man – because by that very fact every man could be Christ, or even, in a certain sense, because, in the depths that are henceforth his own, every human being is taken up by Christ.

In analysing this unusual form of martyrdom, let us not forget

the word 'innocents'. These children are further conformed to
Christ by virtue of the fact that have been guilty of no evil, and are
totally vulnerable before the onslaughts of this 'Herodian' hatred
of God that they incur. They are in the image of the innocent
Lamb led to the slaughter, the Lamb whose innocence and vulner-
ability put to the test all human pretensions to absolute power.
Being as they are the very image of man as heir to Adam, vulnerable by that very fact to the powers of evil without having
participated personally in evil's reality, the Holy Innocents are also
through grace the ones in whom is manifested Christ's victory.

If one accepts that the title of 'martyr' may be given to all those
innocents who are in this way victims of hatred for Christ, it is
certain one can thus bestow this title far beyond the historical situation of the Holy Innocents. In modern totalitarian programmes,
notably, there is an explicit rejection of Christ, a determination to
exclude him so as to construct a sheerly earthly 'new man'. This
refusal of Christ tied as it is to the human claim to allpowerfulness
translates into hatred of all that in man, and especially in his
fragility, transcends these programmes and testifies against them.
In this basis one could perhaps declare 'martyrs' all the innocents
massacred in the Vendée in 1793, burned in the Nazi cremation
ovens, reduced to famine by Lenin in the Ukraine or by Islam in
the southern Sudan, and so forth. One could add to their number
the mentally handicapped eliminated in Nazi programmes of
racial purification. We are faced, it is plain, with plans to eradicate
Christ from human life, plans that, at the hands of men laying
claim to omnipotence, translate immediately into attempts to blot
out human frailty. Nazi anti-Semitism, for example, does not derive
from ancient Christian reactions to so-called 'deicides' but from a
representation of the world, the sacred and the 'superior race' of
which God's historic choice of Israel is the living negation.

Are we able to say the same that clearly about the case of
procured abortion? It is undeniable that, behind the propaganda
which has led to the legalisation of abortion in our Western lands,
there was often concealed a will to promote a 'new look' man.
Pierre Simon, one such propagandist in France, affirms as much in
so many words in his book *L'Homme nouveau ou la mort*: via the
diffusion of contraception and abortion the aim, to his mind, was
to move over from the Christian conception, for which all human
life is sacred, to the Masonic idea for which life is material to be
managed according to rational human requirements.[2] In this sense
one can hardly deny that the spread of abortion in our countries is
linked to explicitly anti-Christian political and social projects.

But does that authorise us to say that *each and every* victim of abortion is a martyr to these undertakings? That would be going too far. True, the decriminalization and legalization of abortion have led to its massive diffusion in practice. However, without letting ourselves be taken in by propaganda giving false figures as to the number of back street abortions, there is no doubt that the problem existed before: certainly not 250,000 clandestine abortions per year, as affirmed by the Institut National de la Statistique et des Etudes économiques on the basis of manipulated figures, and still less the 800,000 claimed by Mme Simone Weil, yet definitely not less than 50,000 (today there are around 300,000 legal and back street abortions per year in France). Then again, one cannot say that all those who voted in favour of the law did so from anti-Christian motives. Many, misled by deceptive propaganda, had motives of an exclusively humanitarian, if naïve, nature (legal abortion was needed so as to avoid 'accidents' owed to lack of medical hygiene, etc.). Finally, with regard to the [pregnant] woman and the medical team concerned: they cannot be said always to act from anti-Christian motives either. At any rate in the majority of cases they seek, surely, only to 'resolve a problem' (comfort, psychological or material distress, and so on) just as they did before the abortion law was passed. In brief, it is impossible to say that *every* aborted child is the victim of an explicitly anti-Christian agenda. Even were it possible, would it not seem strange officially to proclaim as martyrs the victims of abortion after 1974, the year abortion was legalized in France, and to refuse the title to those who came before?

To support the granting of the official title of martyr in the case of abortion's little victims, two considerations have been advanced: First, just as St John the Baptist was a prophetic witness to the commandment, 'Thou shalt not commit adultery', so little ones in the womb of their mother are by their very existence silent witnesses to the commandment, 'Thou shalt not kill'.

Secondly, Satan, 'a murderer from the beginning', is the instigator of all abortion even when those who carry out abortions do not invoke him. These two facts are beyond doubt. But do they suffice to justify the declaration that is at issue? If they did, we would have so extensive a definition of martyrdom that all innocent victims of unjust and murderous violence would have a right to it. The philosopher Emmanuel Levinas has rightly drawn our attention to the fact that every human countenance, in its fragility and nakedness, 'petitions me': that is to say, reverberates in my consciousness by its call on my respect and service. In other words, *every man* is in his very being a silent witness to the commandment, 'thou shalt not kill'. And we are justified in saying that Satan is the inspirer not only of abortions but also of wars, murders and all unjust actions that cause the deaths of innocent people (for example, the economic blockade of Iraq has produced tens of thousands of fatalities among children). Must we then declare all these victims to be 'martyrs'? Even though such a title may shock when used each time a wicked act is committed, are we not going to render commonplace the title of martyr to the point of emptying it of all specific theological content?

Conclusion

After this all too brief *tour d'horizon*, it seems that, at least for the moment, the current state of Church teaching and theology do not permit us to envisage making the declaration at issue. The Church would have to make a prior commitment of her teaching authority on the personal status of the embryo from conception, something she has hitherto refused to do. It would also be necessary for her to clarify the question of children who have died without Baptism, something which, again, she has always avoided. Of course these two preliminaries are by no means impossible of fulfilment. We have seen how a certain set of data can be put forward to help progress in these domains. The third question appears to the present writer the most serious: to put things plainly, the notion of martyrdom should not be watered down to mean the general fact of being the innocent victim of unjust violence. A priori it is not evident how abortion is to be distinguished theologically from other forms that violence takes, forms in whose regard the Church has never considered bestowing the title of martyr. To take the matter further, one would have to enlarge the scope of the definition of martyrdom, and this would carry with it the obvious danger of dissolving martyrdom's specifically Christological reference in the wider pool of the human search for justice. Alternatively, one would have to show in what the fetal victim of abortion finds itself closer to the mystery of Christ than the Albanian child killed by Serbs in Kossovo. Without wanting, since I am not infallible, to foreclose the debate, I admit to not knowing how this difficulty could be overcome.

Supposing, however, that issue from this *impasse* is possible, there remains one more question. Since there are many cases where the liturgical prayer of the Church in its peculiar efficacy has preceded theological reflection and even enabled it, are we not reversing the proper order of things when we wish, contrarywise, to make this reflection come first? This query makes it possible for us to mention a further point, and that is the fruits for the Church of such devotion. It is clear that Church authority would be gravely lacking in prudence if it relied only on the existence of a private revelation in taking a stand. However, in the absence of adequate theological reflection another consideration remains possible: does the declaration sought correspond to a real movement of prayer in the Church with attendant wholesome and authenticated spiritual fruits? In that context, is the Lord himself manifesting in perspicuous, and on occasion miraculous, signs, his will to see the Church recognize officially as martyrs abortion's fetus victims?

If as, so far as my knowledge extends, this does not appear to be the case, we have before us neither an adequate theological reflection nor those 'good fruits' normally produced by a 'good tree', then Church authority lacks the minimum required to commit itself. That I believe to be our present situation. Nothing, however, prevents reflection continuing, and for those who desire such, asking from God the necessary signs pertinent to such a declaration. If the Lord truly wants it, he will give them.

A note on the implications of the title 'martyr'

Up to now, the Church has always reserved the title 'martyr' for those who, in being put to death, have confessed Christ in explicit terms. The need for such explicitness is also verified in the case of 'moral martyrdom': it was explicitly on account of Christ that St Maria Goretti preferred death to carnal sin; it was explicitly because of his prophetic mission that St John the Baptist accused King Herod of sin and underwent death; it was as a Catholic priest that St Maximilian Kolbe was deported by the Nazis and took the place of a man unjustly condemned. This same explicit character is found with the Holy Innocents too, since they died as a result of hatred for Christ.

Why this need for explicitness? The title 'martyr' has an official status in the Church. It signifies 'witness', which means that it makes more visible and evident the fact that divine good things are to be preferred to everything else. Indeed, the object of such witness directly concerns the transcendence of Christ over and above every created good, even the most precious, even that which is most adorned with graces (for human life, even when it is beautified by divine grace, remains something created). 'If anyone

comes to me and does not hate his own father and mother and wife
and children and brothers and sisters, yes, and even his own life,
he cannot be my disciple' (Luke 14:26). This is what the martyr
directly attests by his dying.

Now the simple fact that one speaks of a merely implicit martyrdom shows that what we are concerned with is not primarily Christ
himself but human life: more specifically, the human life of the
child in its mother's womb. Only by virtue of the mystery of grace
and subsequently does one affirm that Christ is identified with this
child. In other words, we get no sense here of the visible, explicit
character of Christ's being preferred to everything else, including
the most precious human life: the focus shifts instead to the *invisible fashion* in which Christ is present, identified by grace with this
[human] life.

These features of implicitness and invisibility thus conflict with
the official title of martyr. There is a risk that, as a consequence,
the transcendence of the good that is Christ in relation to every
desire for justice, even one inspired by charity and the deepest
compassion, will be lost to view.

We should note further, however, that this question of the recognition of martyrdom has to be distinguished from that of the
eternal glorification of the victims of abortion (and consequently
of the eventual possibility of invoking them as intercessors). This
question calls for study and remains open.

Notes

1   J.-H. Nicolas, O.P., *Synthèse dogmatique. De la Trinité à la Trinité*
    (Fribourg: Editions Universitaires, Paris: Beauchesne, 1985), pp. 845,
    853.
2   P. Simon, *L'Homme nouveau ou la mort: théorie unitaire de la connaissance
    et formule de la vie* (Paris: Trédaniel, 1990).

5

The martyr status of the aborted child: a share in Christ's witness to the Father of mercies

Michele M. Schumacher
University of Fribourg, Switzerland

The question of whether aborted children might be considered companion martyrs of the Holy Innocents of Bethlehem is not simply a revisiting of the question of their salvation in light of the Church's insistence upon the necessity of Baptism. If the Lord is capable of raising up children of Abraham from stones (cf. Matt. 3:9), he is certainly 'not bound by his sacraments', as the *Catechism* teaches (no. 1257), which is to say that his omnipotence is a perfect match to his divine benevolence. Indeed, beyond the *Catechism*'s note of 'hope' as regards the salvation of children who have died without Baptism (cf. no. 1261), John Paul II regards aborted children as 'living in the Lord'.[1] Of course a definitive pronouncement is evident in neither case, so it is altogether reasonable that one might try to solve the 'problem' of their salvation by walking in the back door: to claim the children as martyrs is to grant them baptism by blood (cf. no. 1258). The difficulty with this approach – despite its legitimacy – is, it seems to me, that it necessarily focuses upon martyrdom as a shedding of blood and thus obscures the more basic etymological sense of martyrdom as a witness.

The idea of martyrdom, on the other hand, brings us back to an important element of Baptism (whether by water or blood), namely, the conformity of the human person to the divine Person of Christ: an *ontological* conformity (effected by grace) in virtue of which we share in his suffering so as to also share in his glory (Rom. 8:16–17; cf. Rom. 6:3–4; Col. 2:12). This is the reverse formulation of the fact that Christ has taken on our nature so as to share in our suffering (cf. Heb. 4:15). Indeed, such a presentation of salvation as a conformity of Christ is, perhaps, a reformulation of the patristic idea of an *admirabile commercium,* a 'wonderful exchange': the Son of God became the Son of Man in order that by divine adoption, human persons might become children of God.[2] Here too, we confront the mystery expressed by the scholastic tradition as a distinction between objective and subjective redemption according to which there may be said to be an application of the merits of Christ's death by a 'reproduction' *in this particular human being* (subjective redemption) of what Christ accomplished for all (objective redemption). A personal appropriation of the universal gift of salvation (cf. 1 Tim. 2:4), subjective redemption entails that the individual be formed into the likeness of Christ until Christ be formed in him (cf. Gal. 4:19). In other words, the descending mediation of Christ (his assimilation of himself to humanity) continues even in the ascending mediation whereby the human person is changed into his likeness (his assimilation of humanity to himself), which is to say that Christ continues his life and mission within us, even to the extent of suffering and dying 'in' us.

Thus is evident the need to address a further precision: the subjective aspect of redemption entails not merely a reception of the gift of salvation, a welcoming of Christ and a real partaking of his life; it also supposes a real share in the 'work' of salvation, an authentic participation in Christ's redeeming actions whereby he witnesses to the Father. That is to say, such a response to the divine action in our souls (a *received* response) is simultaneously a mediation of grace, a gift for the world, a participation in the very work of redemption as an on-going process. In giving oneself to Christ (as a response to *his* gift, i.e. the gift of his very person in the communication of grace), one is given to the world. To borrow an expression from Origen, one is thereby an 'ecclesial soul'.[3] Through Christ and in Christ, the Christian is, as it were, 'saved and saviour'.[4]

It is here that the case of martyrdom is particularly pungent: the issue remains that of conformity to Christ in his suffering, but a conformity which allows for a mediation of grace, a conformity which gives 'place' to the Spirit's action whereby the martyr's passion is truly a 'witness'. The question of the martyrdom of aborted children concerns not simply their own salvation, but also the salvation of us all, which is to say that their participation in Christ's salvific witness, which is the focal point of our examination, is efficacious for the Church and for the world.

In an attempt to provide an initial response to the Question of whether the aborted child might be considered a martyr, I will argue, firstly, that he benefits from Christ's descending mediation whereby he is mystically identified with him. Beyond this, even in the absence of an operative will, I will defend for his 'mystical' share in Christ's passion (and thus in His 'Passover' to the Father), which is to say that he likewise receives of Christ's ascending mediation. More specifically, I will maintain that by means of his participation in Christ's revelation of sin and of mercy, he is, with Christ, a mediator of salvation. Acknowledging that this participation is largely dependent upon the Church's mediation, I will argue for the significance of her claiming of aborted children in light of her mission to proclaim and to manifest the divine mercy. Finally, I will conclude in admitting that the proclamation of aborted children as martyrs would set a new precedent for martyrdom in general.

An ontological witness to the divine goodness and a mystical identification with Christ

To begin, it bears mention, especially in an increasingly utilitarian culture such as ours – a culture which accords a disproportionate value to action over against being (even to the extent that the former often becomes the condition of the latter) – that existence itself is, as the tradition insists, 'good': *omne ens est bomum*. As divine creations, aborted children – like all human persons – are eternally willed and loved; one might even say 'loved' into being.[5] Hence, the very fact of their existence is itself a natural, ontological (as distinguished from a chosen, willed) witness to the divine benevolence. Indeed, even St Thomas – who denies beatitude to the unborn child due to a lack of reason whereby he is rendered incapable of the acts of faith and charity which unite one to the passion of Christ[6] – would grant that they 'manifest the glory of God, by participating naturally in divine goodness'.[7] Beyond this, one might speak of a 'reply' to the divine call to existence in the very 'act' of being,[8] which is to say that the potentiality ('potency') rightfully attributed to a newly-conceived human being already supposes a primary 'act', i.e. that of 'receiving' being, or that of simply being.[9]

Within such a perspective it is indeed meaningful to speak of a 'dialogue' of salvation between these children and their Creator despite their 'untimely' deaths. On the other hand, given the fact of original sin, one cannot simply equate the gift of being (nature) with that of grace, such that the original communication and reception of the one supposes the other. Hence although the Creator-creature dialogue finds its commencement in the divine call (and the creature's response) to existence, still another invitation (and another response) must be accorded if the dialogue is to be authentically one of 'salvation'. That is to say, to grant that the aborted child really *receives* salvation is, in a sense, to grant that salvation is not necessarily communicated with the gift of (physical/natural) life (which is nonetheless in the divine image), or to acknowledge the real necessity of his redemption by Christ. As participants in a dialogue of salvation which finds its commencement in their creation *by* the divine Word and *in* the divine Word (i.e. in the image of the Only-Begotten Son), aborted children, like all human persons, are distinguished from other created things which also witness to the divine goodness without imaging the divine Word. By the Incarnation of that same Word in Mary's womb, moreover, they benefit of his sanctifying presence there (cf. Luke 1:44). That is to say, the patristic witness to the full humanity of Christ – *quod non assumptum non est sanctum* (that which is not assumed is not sanctified) – is positively formulated in that the unborn baby partakes of the sanctifying graces which abound in that sanctuary of life, the holy place of conception.[10]

Here the descending mediation of Christ is particularly apparent: the primary *kenosis* (cf. Phil. 2:6–7) of the eternal Word, his assumption of human flesh, is the principle of his mystical identification with each human person.[11] Hence, with specific reference to the child in the womb, John Paul II speaks of the 'opportunity to serve Jesus' in accord with his own words: 'As you did it to one of the least of these my brethren, you did it to me' (Matt. 25:40).[12] Similarly, an 'attack' on these little ones is, he insists, an attack on Christ, as in the case of the first Holy Innocents: 'it is precisely in the "flesh" of every person that Christ continues to reveal himself and to enter into fellowship with us, so that *rejection of human life*, in whatever form that rejection takes, *is really a rejection of Christ.* This is the fascinating but also demanding truth which Christ reveals to us and which his Church continues untiringly to proclaim.'[13]

This descending mediation of the eternal Word is, however, only 'half' the equation of humanity's salvation: for Christ's identification with the 'least of these' is that which effects their identification with him, that whereby they share in his predestination as 'sons in the Son' and that whereby they are granted a real share in his 'Passover' to the Father. To return to the important patristic formulation, the salvific mysteries are those of an *admirabile commercium.* Hence, to regard the aborted child as a martyr is to suppose not merely that Christ represents him, but also that *he represents Christ*, or better, that he shares in Christ's own witness, as the revelation of the Father and of his merciful love.

The 'martyrdom' of the aborted child: the status of the question

Without begging the question of his martyrdom, it is certainly reasonable to argue (especially in light of Christ's descending mediation) that the aborted child shares in Christ's witness as a sign, or 'sacrament', of the spotless Lamb of God led to the slaughter (cf. Isa. 53:7; Acts 8:32; John 1:29, 36; Rev. 5:6; 13:8, etc.). In the innocent suffering of the aborted infant, the crucifixion of the unblemished Lamb is powerfully imaged. Still more is implied, however, in granting to this child a real share in Christ's passion which realizes his conformity to Christ, whereby he, like St Paul, might be said to bear on his tiny body the 'marks of Jesus' (Gal. 6:17) so as to carry 'in the body' the death of Jesus. 'For while we live we are always being given up to death for Jesus' sake, so that the life of Jesus may be manifested in our mortal flesh' (cf. 2 Cor. 4:11; cf. v. 10).

What lies in the balance here, it seems to me, is the question of what may be expressed as that 'second degree' of the human creature's likeness to God whereby the 'truth' of his creation in the image of the Son is expressed in his actions or even in his lack thereof, in what we might refer to as his 'passion'.[14] In other words, the 'image of God' in the human person is realized not only as a gift, but also as a task,[15] as is apparent in the patristic commentaries of Genesis 1:27, which accord to the term 'image' (*selem*) the value of 'nature' while 'likeness' (*demut*) is recognized as 'assimilation'.[16] In Thomistic terms, the first degree of likeness, accorded in virtue of creation in the Word (the creature's *exitus* from the Creator), is to be complemented, or completed, by the second: the creature's *reditus* to the Creator.[17] Given the reality of sin and death, this *reditus* is effected by Christ's own Passover to the Father as a share in his suffering: '(...) we are children of God, and if children, then heirs, heirs of God and fellow heirs with Christ, provided we suffer with him in order that we may also be glorified with him' (Rom. 8:16–17).

In the case of aborted children, we might ask, then, whether this second 'degree' of likeness is accorded in the absence of reason, and thus without their willing cooperation. More specifically, might they somehow participate in the work of salvation (their own and/or that of others) without consciously doing so? Given the precedent of the Holy Innocents of Bethlehem, such a likeness is easily granted in the case of martyrdom, which is to say both that martyrdom conforms one to Christ and that this conformity in death and suffering does not require a conscious self gift.[18] Since it is the very status of martyrdom which is in question in the case of aborted children, however, it is worthwhile posing still another question. Again, the issue is obviously not whether God can save the aborted child without his assent, but whether or not his life and his 'untimely' death are a witness to the Lord and to his truth, or better, whether these are a share in Christ's witness to the Father of mercies.

A share in Christ's salvific witness?

To be sure, there is no clear separation between the receptive and the active phase of our (subjective) redemption just as there is no clear separation between a mystical doctrine of salvation – according to which Christ is presented, for example, as a 'redeemer in the womb'[19] – and the presentation of the Cross as the source of our salvation. For, whereas our actions are effective towards salvation because they are rooted in Christ (cf. John 15:4), his actions are salvific in virtue of the hypostatic union whereby, as St Cyril (d. 444) argued, the body of Christ is united to life itself and in this way becomes a dispenser of life.[20] As both the author of grace and its subject, he is simultaneously our salvation (emphasis on being) and our saviour (emphasis on action). Hence, his witness to the Father is achieved in both respects. On the one hand, his 'works' testify to the Father.[21] On the other hand – indeed, more profoundly – his very *being* is a witness to the Father who sent him: '... what he spoke before to the prophets in parts, he has now spoken all at once by giving us the All Who is His Son.'[22] Christ does not merely speak the words of the Father (cf. John 8: 28; 12:49; 14:10); he *is* the Word of the Father. Similarly – indeed, as a privileged participant in Christ's supreme witness to the Father and to his love – the martyr's 'own' witness is effective in word and action only because he or she is ontologically rooted (i.e. by grace) in the very being of him who is 'one' with the Father (cf. John 10:30).[23] In virtue of his *ontological conformity to Christ* (as effected by grace), the martyr *participates in his life-giving actions*, especially and ultimately in his sorrowful Passion. In the case of

Baptism by blood, the conformity is effected in the participation itself, which in no way denies that his witness remains deeply rooted in Christ.[24]

To accord the martyr's palm to the aborted child is to grant not only that he bears Christ's (crucified) image in himself, but also that he *mediates* Christ's life (and this, in the gift of his own life, even unto death). With reference to the etymological meaning of the word *martyr*, it is supposed that he bears witness (implicitly or explicitly) to Christ (and/or to the moral order)[25] thereby engaging others in this same dialogue of salvation. Or, to return to the parallel with Christ as substantial grace and source of that grace by which we share his divine life, it is supposed that his share in Christ's Passion is efficacious not only for himself, but also for others (and ultimately for the Church). That is to say, he is thought to share in Christ's mediating function (cf. 2 Tim. 2:5) whereby Christ draws others into his own sonship, his privileged relationship with the Father (cf. Eph. 1:5–6). Thus the blood of St Stephen – who, despite the testimony of the Holy Innocents, is often regarded as the first Christian martyr – is presented by Luke as mediating the graces of St Paul's conversion (cf. Acts 7:58; 8:1) particularly in his inspired prayer: 'Lord, do not hold this sin against them' (7:60; cf. Luke 23:34).

Here we are confronted with a theology of the Cross which, far from vindicating divine 'justice' by calming the Father's anger, might be best understood as a giving without turning back, an enduring love which holds on to the bitter end, an almost obstinate refusal to withdraw the gift of one's life to and for the beloved, which is to say, the willing acceptance of the consequences of that initial and on-going gift of God himself to his people (i.e. the gift of the Incarnation), given the authenticity of their freedom. In other words, such a theology regards the sorrowful passion of Jesus as a witness, not so much to the severity of the divine countenance, as to the unbounded character of the Father's love.[26]

The aborted child's share in Christ's revelation of sin and mercy

If one interprets the meaning of Christ's Passion in negative terms – as non-resistance vis-à-vis the violent attacks which claim his life – then one might argue for the aborted child's share in the same: his innocence with regard to evil – indeed, his absolute inability to protect himself from it[27] – allows for no perpetuation of violence.[28]

Because such a perpetuation may be understood as the outgrowth of original sin, moreover, his innocence might be thought to contribute to its reversal: to not perpetuate the cycle of violence is to effectively help in stopping it.[28] Certainly this may be understood in minimalist terms as not falling prey to the lure of sin whereby the victim of today becomes the aggressor of tomorrow, violence begetting violence.[30] More positively, however, it may be considered as a share in Christ's mystic function of *revealing* both *sin* and *mercy*.

With regard to the first revelation (i.e. that of sin), Christ's refusal to return violence for violence (cf. Matt. 5:38–48) becomes the means whereby the sin of those who condemned and crucified him is, as it were, absorbed into his flesh. The innocent Lamb of God who remains so to the bitter end – without succumbing to evil in any respect – becomes the perfect 'scapegoat' of sinful humanity: 'He was oppressed, and he was afflicted, yet he opened not his mouth: like a lamb that is led to the slaughter, and like a sheep that before its shearers is dumb, so he opened not his mouth' (Is. 53:7). The 'fruits' of sin – anger, pain, hatred, etc. – are thus, as it were, 'taken on' by him to be driven away: 'he has borne our griefs and carried out sorrows (...) he was cut off out of the land of the living, stricken for the transgression of my people' (vv. 4, 8). On the other hand, the flesh which 'bears' these sins, becomes a sort of 'revelation' of the misery of man, the state of humanity's abasement. 'He was despised and rejected by men; a man of sorrows, acquainted with grief; and as one from whom men hide their faces he was despised, and we esteemed him not' (v. 3). Indeed, mystics have recognized in Christ crucified the manifestation of sin: his bloodied and thorn-crowned head reveals the state of man's pride; his naked body reveals the sins of man's extravagance and concupiscence; the imprints of the nails which held him fast reveal the extent of man's licentiousness, the perfect abuse of his liberty. Is this not echoed in the significant formulation of John Paul II that '*every sin* wherever and whenever committed has a reference to the Cross of Christ – and therefore indirectly also to the sin of those who "have not believed in him", and who condemned Jesus Christ to death on the Cross'?[31]

More specifically, to return to the question of the aborted child and his partaking of Christ's redemptive mission, it may be argued that his own 'passion' may be efficacious in sensitizing the consciences of those responsible for the horrendous crime claiming his life. In this respect, it is worth mention that the progressive obscuring of consciences with regard to abortion – its acceptance 'in popular mind, in behaviour and even in law itself', and this, despite what John Paul II describes as the 'inviolability' of life which is 'written from the beginning in man's heart' – reveals a 'structure of sin' so profound as to cause a moral crisis characterized by the incapacity to distinguish between good and evil.[32] Precisely because there is no retaliation of the crime of abortion, its victims are particularly effective in confronting this 'structure': their innocence does not allow for confusion as regards guilt, which is to say that – even despite the disproportionate emphasis in contemporary feminist discourse, for instance, upon a woman's 'right' to her body – they simply cannot be mistaken for aggressors. Might not the words which John Paul II applies to martyrs thus be applied to them: '(...) they are a living reproof to those who transgress the law (cf. Wis. 2:12), and they make the words of the prophet echo ever afresh: "Woe to those who call evil good and good evil ..."' (Isa. 5:20)?[33] Indeed, we might argue that in virtue of his innocent suffering, the aborted child shares in the power of Christ's absolutely unique sacrifice to open the door of consciences to the action of the Holy Spirit whose 'convincing concerning sin' (i.e. in reference to the Cross) enables the conversion whereby one is, in turn, open to the gift of forgiveness, the remission of sins.[34]

This 'convincing concerning sin' implies not merely the gift of 'the truth of conscience' but also that of 'the certainty of redemption.'[35] That is to say, the redemptive power of the Cross is not to be understood in terms of justice, but also and especially in terms of mercy. 'Believing in the crucified Son means "seeing the Father", means believing that love is present in the world and that his love is more powerful than any kind of evil in which individuals, humanity, or the world are involved.'[36] Indeed, Christ's Passion is not merely the result of his refusal to resist evil. It is also, and especially, an absolute gift of himself, even unto death: 'No one takes my life from me, but I lay it down of my own accord. I have power to lay it down, and I have power to take it again' (John 10:18). 'Christ, precisely as the crucified one, (...) stands at the door and knocks at the heart of every man (cf. Rev. 3:20)' inviting him to exercise mercy upon his God through an act of repentant love. '[I]n obtaining mercy, he is in a sense the one who at the same time "shows mercy"',[37] which is to say that he thereby grants 'efficacy' to the sufferings of Christ in the subjective sense: through his willing acceptance of the fruits of Christ's sacrifice, he assures that this sacrifice be not 'in vain' (i.e. in his regard).

Here it is particularly evident that the revelation of sin is only half of the equation expressing the power of the Cross to open consciences to the Spirit's action. Indeed the revelation of sin is of little consequence in the absence of *a revelation of infinite mercy* which encourages the prodigal's return. Thus, as if to reverse the cry of Abel's innocent blood for vengeance (Gen. 4:10) from which ensues a terrible circle of violence, Christ's blood cries out instead for forgiveness: 'This is my blood of the covenant, which is poured out for many for the forgiveness of sins' (Matt. 26:28).[38] Similarly (indeed, by the power of the same), the martyr's love for his enemy – as in Stephen's repetition of Christ's prayer for forgiveness (Acts 7:60: cf. Luke 23:34) – is a revelation of divine mercy.

The meaning of the Church's claiming of aborted children: a manifestation of mercy

Certainly the children killed by abortion are unable willingly to give their lives, in union with Christ, as an offering for sin and thus as a means of conversion and forgiveness. On the other hand, without begging the question at hand, it seems to me that the Church might and perhaps even ought to do so. That is to say, if it is truly into *her* faith that we are baptized – and this even when our faith is weak at best – and if, moreover, she has really been granted the power to say, 'your sins are forgiven you' (cf. John 20:23), then might not the Church plead that the short lives and the dreadful deaths of these children be united to the meritorious life and Death of Christ for their own salvation and for that of the world? Rather than leaving their unavenged blood to fill the cup of divine wrath (cf. Isa. 51:17; Rev. 14:10; 16:19), might she not grant that it be mingled with the cup of Christ's blood for the world's redemption? She who offers our humanity in Christ's eucharistic sacrifice in the mingling of the water and wine, might she not likewise offer their blood to the eternal Father with that of Jesus for the forgiveness of sins? In the significant formulation of Saint Faustina, might not the Church plead, 'for the sake of their sorrowful passion, have mercy on us and on the whole world'? Indeed, since John Paul II has encouraged mothers of aborted children to ask forgiveness from their children,[39] is it unreasonable to think that these same children might be powerful intercessors before God and the Lamb for the forgiveness of their mothers and of all whose hands and souls are stained by their blood? More specifically, might not the Church give meaning to their lives and to their untimely deaths in just such a plea of mercy?[40] To acknowledge these children as martyrs is not merely to grant them a share in this mercy by giving them a home in the Church: it is to make of them ambassadors of mercy and mediators of salvation. Such, it seems to me, is, in the final analysis, the meaning of the Church's intervention in raising these children to the altars.

The martyrdom of the aborted child: a new precedent

The Church's proclamation of aborted children as martyrs despite their incapacity to willingly offer their lives is, of course, not without precedent. Is this not evident in claiming them as companions of the Holy Innocents of Bethlehem? We cannot deny, however, that their witness, unlike that of Bethlehem's infants, is not directly *to Christ*. In the Church's claiming of Maximilian Kolbe, on the other hand, we have another precedent upon which to rest our case: that of the martyrdom of charity. It is not explicitly for Christ that the martyr of Auschwitz dies, but for his neighbour in whom he recognizes Christ. Rather than witnessing *to Christ*, Kolbe willingly allows Christ to witness, *in him*, to the love of God.

Given these two examples, the question concerning aborted children might be rephrased as whether – in the absence, not only of (operative) reason, but also of an explicit witness to Christ – they might be considered martyrs. More specifically, I am asking whether the Magisterium might offer their lives, their suffering and their deaths in union with those of Christ for the world's salvation, beginning with that of their murderers. To do so, is, first of all, to propose a certain role of the Magisterium which might be misunderstood as a begging of the question: it might seem that the Church, in her active offering of the blood of these children who cannot offer it themselves, actually *creates* martyrs rather than merely acknowledging them as such. On the other hand, it would seem that her offering of their blood is in perfect accord with her mission to distribute the graces of the paschal mysteries entrusted to her safekeeping. Secondly, the Church's intervention would, it must be admitted, open the same possibility to other truly innocent victims of violent crimes – children who have not reached the age of reason and the mentally handicapped, for instance – victims whose blood, when offered by the Church with that of Christ, might truly 'speak more graciously than the blood of Abel' (cf. Heb. 12:24) to convict the consciences of those responsible for the violent taking of their lives thereby allowing for the penetration of the graces of conversion for all those involved in the horrendous crime of abortion. On the other hand, given the magnitude of the crime of abortion and the obscuring of 'public' conscience in its regard, there is, it seems to me, a certain urgency which would advocate their cause at this moment in history even before that of other truly innocent victims.

Notes

1   John Paul II, Encyclical Letter on the Gospel of Life, *Evangelium Vitae*, n. 99.

2   'Propter hoc enim Verbum dei homo, et qui Filius Dei est Filius hominis factus est ut homo, commixtus Verbo dei et adoptionem percipiens, fiat filius Dei' (St Irenaeus, *Adversus Haereses* III.19.1; *Sources chrétiennes* n. 211, p. 374.)

3   See Hans Urs von Balthasar, 'Who is the Church' in *Spouse of the Word*, vol. 2 of *Explorations in Theology* (San Francisco: Ignatius Press, 1991), p. 173.

4   'ex uno et per unum et servantur et servant' (Clement of Alexandria, *Stromatum* VI.2; PG Vol. 9 col. 414).

5   See Thomas Aquinas, S. Th. I, q. 5, a.1; Josef Pieper: 'Verteidigungsrede für die Philosophie' in *Werke* III. (Hamburg: Felix Meiner, 1995), p. 108; *idem*, 'Über die Liebe', *Werke* IV (Hamburg: Felix Meiner, 1997), pp. 320–21; p. 326; Kenneth L Schmitz. *The Gift: Creation* [The Aquinas Lecture, 1982] (Maidson: Marquette University Press, 1982), p. 92; John Paul II, 'Letter To Families' (February 2, 1994), no. 9.

6   See S. Th. III.q. 52, a.7.

7   B. Guallier, *L'état des enfants morts sans baptême d'après saint Thomas d'Aquin* (Paris: Lethielleux, 1962), p. 137. St Thomas argues that unbaptized children 'will in nowise grieve for being deprived of the divine vision, nay, rather, they will rejoice that they will have a large share of God's goodness and their own natural perfections.' (*In* II *Sent.*, d.33, q. 2, a.1). This, Christopher Beiting argues, follows as a consequence, in Thomas' reasoning, of the fact that 'one cannot grieve the loss of that which one was not meant naturally to have, any more than normal people grieve because they do not have wings or are not kings.' (C. Beiting, 'Limbo in Thomas Aquinas', *The Thomist* 62 [1998], pp. 240–41).

8   Cf. Thomas Aquinas, *Summa contra Gentiles*, II.c.54 (3) and S. Th. I, q. 5, a.1, ad 1. Schmitz argues that within the Thomistic perspective, being is, in and of itself, considered act: 'we name things *being* because they are *in act* (*esse in actu*)', (op cit., p. 99; cf. S. Th. I, q. 5, a.1 ad 1: *Contra Gentiles* II.c.54, 3). Schmitz explains that 'in calling a being *actual*, we name it in virtue of its active principle, its agency.' In simple terms, 'act means neither *fact* nor *result*, but *principle*' (op. cit., pp. 102, 103).

9   Even in the case of creation *ex nihilo*, there is, as Schmitz argues, an

'endowment of the capacity to receive being in the very communication in which that actually is being received.' ('Created Receptivity and the Philosophy of the Concrete,' *The Thomist* 61, n. 3 [July 1977], 359.) 'Of course, because the creative offer of being is absolutely radical, it would be quite wrong to imagine that, before the offer is actually made, the creature waits in some state of possibility in order to accept or reject the gift. For the recipient of that radical gift only comes into being with it. No creature is consulted before it is created, because there is no creature to consult. (...) Still, we are justified in speaking of creation as an offer. For it is freely given being, a sort of ontological credit advanced for subsequent realization in and through the career of the creature.' (Schmitz, *The Gift*, op. cit., p. 93).

10 Augustine, for example, presents the Virgin's womb as a wedding chamber in which is united the eternal Word and human nature: 'Verbum enim sponsus et sponsa caro humana; et utrumque unus Filius Dei, et idem filius hominis: ubi factus est caput Ecclesiae, ille uterus virginis Mariae thalamus ejus, inde processit tanquam sponsus de thalamo suo (...)' (*In Joannis Evangelium* VII, 2. 4: *Homélies sur l'Évangile de Saint Jean* [Bibliothèque Augustinienne, 71]. Paris: Desclée de Brouwer, 1969, pp. 474–476: PL 35:1452).

11 See Vatican II, Pastoral Constitution on the Church, *Gaudium et Spes*, n. 22.

12 See *Evangelium Vitae*, n. 87.

13 *Ibid.*, n. 104. Here reference is made, once again, to Mt. 25:40, as well as to Mt. 18:5 ('Whoever receives one such child in my name receives me').

14 Here it is worth noting the distinction between *passion* and *action*, the former referring not primarily to what one *does* but to what *is done unto*: what is endured, suffered or received: in a positive sense – grace, divine sonship, etc – in a negative sense: injury even unto death.

15 To take an example as a case in point, Mary conceived without sin, is the negative formulation of the fact that she is conceived in grace, and thus a child of God from the first moment of her conception. She does not, however, witness to her sanctity (and thus to the marvellous work of the Lord in her soul for her salvation and for the salvation of the world) primarily in her abstinence with regard to sin, but rather in her actions and ultimately in her maternal 'passion'. In the unconditional gift of herself to the Lord for his saving purpose, we observe both the work of God in her soul and her response. Because she is simultaneously conceived and redeemed, however, she is redeemed without her consent, which is obviously not to deny that her fiat is really required of her, not only for herself, but for the world. Indeed, the exceptional gift of Mary (the Immaculate Conception) is ordered to her divine maternity, to the salvific event of the Incarnation and all that follows therefrom, which is not to deny the fact that she is really loved in an exceptional manner, as is befitting her maternal role with respect to Son of God.

16 Such as the case of Irenaeus, Origen, Basil and Maximus the
    Confessor. See Hans Urs von Balthasar, *Theo-Drama: Theological
    Dramatic Theory*, vol. 2: *Dramatic Personae: Man in God* (San Francisco:
    Ignatius Press, 1992), p. 318, pp. 327–30.

17 Hence the formulation of St John 'Beloved you are God's children
    now, it does *not yet* appear what we shall be' (1 Jn. 3:2a). It is worth
    mentioning that even in the case of the terrestrial paradise of Eden,
    the human person did not enjoy the full beatific vision, although he
    did possess a greater ability to perceive God than fallen man. See
    Thomas Aquinas, S. Th. I, q. 95, a.3.

18 See St Thomas's classification of martyrs in the *Supplement* to the
    S. Th., q. 96, a.6, obj. 3 and ad 12.

19 See John Saward, *Redeemer in the Womb: Jesus Living in Mary* (San
    Francisco: Ignatius Press, 1993).

20 Cf. Thomas: 'Sed gratia non derivatur a Christo in nos mediante
    natura humana, sed per solam personalem actionem ipsius Christi.
    Unde non opertet in Christo distinguere duplicem gratiam, quarum
    una respondeat naturae, alia personae ...' (S. Th. III, q. 8 a.5. ad 1)
    See also III, q. 7 a.1 ad 3: q. 8 a.1 ad 1: q. 43 a.2: q. 48 a 6.

21 This is a recurring theme in John's Gospel. See 5:36: 9:4: 10:25, 32,
    37–38; 14:10–11; 15:24.

22 St John of the Cross, *The Ascent of Mount Carmel*, 2. 22. 3–5: cited in *The
    Catechism of the Catholic Church*, no. 65. Cf. Heb. 1:1–2.

23 As the means whereby the human person shares in the divine nature,
    the grace of adoption is the principle of his collaboration in the prop-
    erly divine work of Redemption (cf. I–II, q. 110, a.4, a.2).

24 That is to say, the logical priority remains in what may be regarded as
    a temporal simultaneity.

25 See John Paul II, Encyclical letter 'On the Splendour of Truth',
    Veritatis Splendor, n. 93.

26 Hence the 'command' (*entolê*: Jn. 10:17–18; 12–49–51) which the Son
    receives from the Father is not primarily that of justifying humanity
    before God by taking on its punishment for sin, thereby reversing
    Adam's refusal of God through his (Christ's) own filial obedience
    Rather, the command and the mission consist, I believe, in this: that
    the Son return *to* the Father with the world for whose sake he came
    forth on mission *from* the Father (cf. Jn. 3:13–16: 1 Jn. 4:16; etc.). That
    is to say, it is a command to deliver, or surrender, his life (cf. Phil. 2:6;
    Jn. 5:21) along with the Father's love for him (Jn. 10:18; 12:49, 50;
    14:31) to those to whom he is sent by the Father. Hence there is
    implied a eucharistic surrender which is positively formulated as a
    communication or sharing of the divine nature, a pouring forth *in time*
    of the divine 'substance' (cf. Jn. 6:53, 55) which is eternally poured
    forth in itself (i.e. in its triune union) so as to be mysteriously identi-
    fied with this constant dynamism of giving and receiving. More
    specifically within the context of sin and the resistance which it neces-
    sarily implies, it consists in the gift of unconditional forgiveness: 'For

this is my blood of the covenant, which is to be poured out for many for the forgiveness of sins' (Mt. 26:28). Whereas Abel's blood had cried out to the Lord for vengeance (Gen. 4:10), Christ's blood cries out for reconciliation (Heb. 12:24–25). See my article. 'The Concept of Representation in the Theology of Hans Urs von Balthasar,' *Theological Studies* 60 (1999), pp. 53–71.

27 'No one more absolutely *innocent* could ever be imagined. In no way could this human being ever be considered an aggressor, much less an unjust aggressor! He or she is *weak*, defenceless, even to the point of lacking that minimal form of defence consisting in the poignant power of a newborn baby's cries and tears. The unborn child is *totally entrusted* to the protection and care of the woman carrying him or her in the womb.' (*Evangelium Vitae*, no. 58).

28 It is perhaps worth noting that abortion is itself a good example of such a perpetuation. The mother of the aborted child is often herself a victim who chooses abortion as the only way 'out' of what she perceives as a hopeless situation.

29 See John Paul II, Apostolic Exhortation 'On Reconciliation and Penance in the Mission of the Church Today', *Reconciliatio et Paenitentia*, no. 16.

30 See Dominique Barthélemy, *God and His Image: An Outline of Biblical Theology*, translated by Aldhelm Dean (New York: Sheed and Ward, 1966), pp. 171, 174–75.

31 John Paul II, Encyclical Letter 'On the Holy Spirit in the Life of the Church and the World', *Dominum et Vivificatem*, no. 29. Indeed, beyond a simple manifestation of sin, 'the cross of Christ on Calvary is also a witness to the strength of evil against the very Son of God, against the one who, alone among all the sons of men, was by His nature absolutely innocent and free from sin, and whose coming into the world was untainted by the disobedience of Adam and the inheritance of original sin' (*idem*, Encyclical letter 'On the Depths of Mercy', *Dives in Misericordia*, no. 8).

32 See *Evangelium Vitae*, nos. 59, 40, 58. It is worth mentioning, moreover, that 'The good to be done is not added to life as a burden which weighs on it, since the very purpose of life is that good and only by doing it can life be built up' (*ibid.*, no. 48). Hence, this confusion between good and evil is identified as 'the most dangerous crisis which can afflict man' (*ibid.*, no. 93). So too, the Council addressed abortion among other crimes against life as doing 'more harm to those who practice them than those who suffer from the injury' (*Gaudium et Spes*, n. 16).

33 *Veritatis Splendor*, no. 93.

34 *Domininum et Vivificantem*, nos. 44, 45; cf. no. 32. Forgiveness of sin, it is worth noting, implies 'inner contrition' as well as 'sincere and firm purpose of amendment' (no. 42). '*The Holy Spirit "comes"* by virtue of Christ's "departure" in the Paschal Mystery: he comes *in each concrete case of conversion-forgiveness*, by virtue of the sacrifice of the Cross.' (no. 45).

[35] *Ibid.*, no. 32.

[36] *Dives in Misericordia* no. 7.

[37] *Ibid.*, no. 8. Emphasis mine. Similarly, Thomas argues that Christ's passion is the proper cause of the forgiveness of sins not only by way of redemption (i.e. as Head he delivers his members) and by way of efficiency (such that his humanity is the instrument of his divinity), but also by exciting our charity, by which we procure pardon. In coming to know the price of our salvation, we are not only encouraged to refrain from sin, but are also stirred to love God in return for having 'died for us while we were still sinners' (Rom. 5:8). Hence the Cross is deemed necessary for removing those obstacles which precluded us from securing the effects of Christ's merits which began at the time of his conception. See S. Th. III, q. 49, a.1; q. 46, a.3; q. 48, a.1 ad 2.

[38] Cf. Heb. 12:24–25. See also D. Barthélemy, *God and His Image*, op. cit., pp. 177–178; cf. p. 170. 'Precisely because it is poured out as the gift of life, the blood of Christ is no longer a sign of death, of definitive separation from the brethren, but the instrument of communion which is richness of life for all' (*Evangelium Vitae* no. 25).

[39] *Evangelium Vitae*, no. 99.

[40] 'At no time and in no historical period – especially at a moment as critical as our own – can the Church forget *the prayer that is a cry for the mercy of God* amid the many forms of evil which weigh upon humanity and threaten it. Precisely this is the fundamental right and duty of the Church in Christ Jesus, her right and duty towards God and towards humanity. The more the human conscience succumbs to secularization, loses its sense of the very meaning of the word "mercy," moves away from God and distances itself from the mystery of mercy, the more *the Church has the right and the duty* to appeal to the God of mercy "with loud cries."' (*Dives in Misericordia*, no. 15).

6

'Associated with this Paschal Mystery': *Gaudium et Spes* 22, Tradition, the Magisterium and the question at hand

Hugh Barbour, O. Praem.
St. Michael's Abbey, Orange, California

I. The general context for the discussion of human salvation outside of the visible sacraments: *Gaudium et Spes* 22.

Cum enim pro omnibus mortuus sit Christus, cumque vocatio hominis ultima revera una sit, scilicet divina, tenere debemus Spiritum Sanctum cunctis possibilitatem offere ut, modo Deo cognito, huic paschali mysterio consocientur.[1]

Since Christ died for all men, and since the ultimate vocation of man is in fact one, and divine, we ought to believe that the Holy Spirit in a manner known only to God offers to every man the possibility of being associated with this Paschal Mystery.

This solemn statement of the Vatican Council presents four key doctrines which may guide our discussion of the question at hand, and indicate which resolutions are more compatible with the Church's teaching. The **first** doctrine is the universal salvific will of God, which excludes no human individual from its scope: *tenere debemus Spiritum Sanctum cunctis possibilitatem offere.* The **second** doctrine is that the end or calling of man in which his salvation consists is concretely one, *revera una,* and is the work of God himself, is *divina.* The **third** is that the salvific will of God is accomplished by a *consociatio* of the human person with the Paschal Mystery of the incarnate Word, a doctrine even more clearly taught earlier in the same paragraph of *Gaudium et Spes* where it reads *Filius Dei incarnatione sua cum omni homine quodammodo se univit:* 'the

Son of God, by his Incarnation united himself in a certain way with every man'. This statement teaches that in some way at least – *quodammodo* – this *consociatio* is already a fact on some level for each man in virtue of the Lord's Incarnation. The **fourth** is not so much a doctrine as a doctrinal limitation, namely, that the Church does not profess to know the precise manner in which this *consociatio* is a possibility in each case: *modo Deo cognito.*

The particular dogmatic problem which is undoubtedly the general context for this statement and the doctrines it contains, is the Church's awareness that she knows of no other certain means to personal salvation than the sacraments of faith, and primarily the sacrament of Baptism, and that she nonetheless is bound to profess God's universal salvific will for men. These truths are always to be kept in mind as the sure points of reference for any understanding of the less ordinary ways of salvation, which must in any case be resolved to these dogmas. The dogmas regarding the necessity of Baptism and the will of God that all men be saved are the certain principles which shed light on the extraordinary cases, and not the converse. This dogmatic context of the statement in *Gaudium et Spes* 22 is a key one, for it both provides the problem and guides its solution.

The first doctrine tends to rule out a restricted, merely generic interpretation of the universal salvific will. This interpretation, usually identified with the teaching of St Augustine, would interpret the universal salvific will as meaning the non-exclusion of awareness with certainty, other than the fact that this possibility exists and that it is a concretely real one for each human person. A prudent reserve will thus characterize our assertions about extraordinary cases and the extent to which they can be judged by the Magisterium of the Church.

The answer to the question proposed for this consultation will indicate how the teaching of the Second Vatican Ecumenical Council found in *Gaudium et Spes* 22 may be applied in the case of children killed by abortion: *Is there a possible mode of accomplishing a 'consociatio' to the Lord's death proper to the experience of those killed in their mothers' wombs, or does this differ accidentally among them?* More precisely, can this *consociatio* be by way of martyrdom *in odium fidei* as is proposed? If so, can this apply to all of the aborted (in which case the answer to the *first* part of the disjunction would be affirmative) or is it a possibility only for some of them (in which case the answer to the *second* part of the disjunction would be affirmative)? If the second part of the disjunction is answered affirmatively, then the more general case of children who die in their mothers' wombs for other reasons would seem to apply to some of the aborted, and would thus require discussion as providing a defining contrast to the case of those who could be martyrs.

The resolution of these questions will make evident to what extent the Magisterium of the Church might make a declaration regarding the manner in which the aborted unborn enjoy a *consociatio* with the Paschal Mystery.

II. The possibility of the justification of unborn children by Baptism of blood.

There is no question that the taking of the life of an unborn child *in odium fidei* constitutes a genuine martyrdom and a Baptism of blood. This mode of justification exceeds sacramental Baptism in its efficacy, insofar as the conformity to Christ which it accomplishes is 'real,' and so has no need of a sign to convey the reality of a conformity which is evident to the senses. To be sure, the Baptism of blood does not convey anything which pertains strictly to the sacramental order, but it conveys in an eminent manner that which the sacramental sign represents, namely, a *consociatio* to the Paschal Mystery in which human salvation and sanctification consist. St Gregory Nazianzen provides us with the passage, evidently adapted from the teaching of Origen in his second homily on Leviticus, which became the non-Augustinian *locus classicus* as an authority for this doctrine, coming to us practically *verbatim* through St John Damascene to St Thomas and the Latin tradition generally.[2] This Father knows of five kinds[3] of Baptism, that of Moses in the Red Sea, John's baptism, the Baptism of Jesus, the Baptism of blood or martyrdom, *which is also a baptism of Jesus*, and the baptism of penance for sins committed after baptism:

> I know also of a fourth kind of Baptism, that of martyrdom and, blood, that baptism with which Christ himself was baptised, and which is all the more venerable than the others because it cannot be sullied by later faults.[4]

St Gregory of Nyssa in his *Catechetical Oration* provides us with a passage which, although only implicitly referring to martyrdom, directly compares and prefers death for Christ's sake to sacramental baptism. Speaking of the one to be baptized, St Gregory asserts:

Had it been possible for him in his imitation to undergo a complete dying, the result would not be imitation, but identity; and the evil of our nature would so entirely vanish that, as the Apostle says, 'he would die unto sin once for all'. But since as has been said we only so far imitate the transcendent Power as the poverty of our nature is capable of, by having the water thrice poured on us and ascending again up from the water, we enact that saving burial and resurrection which took place on the third day, with this thought in our mind, that as we have power over the water both to be in it and to arise out of it, so he too, who has the universe at his sovereign disposal, immersed himself in death, as we in the water, to return to his own blessedness.[5]

Both the passages from the two Gregories not only extol Baptism of blood insofar as it is a particularly perfect conformity to the death of Christ, but also because of its preeminently efficacious power to render sin a *physical* impossibility through bodily death. This latter insight will be of great importance when we consider the question of the death and fate of unbaptized infants more generally.

This common doctrine of the Greek Fathers is presented concisely, without omitting any of the formal *rationes* which contribute to its understanding and formulation, by St Thomas Aquinas in *In IV Sent. d.4, q.3, qla 4:*

> ... *Baptismus aquae conformat ei sacramentali significatione, baptismus autem sanguinis realiter; ideo quantum ad sacramentalia excedit baptismus aquae, sicut et impressio characteris et huiusmodi; quantum ad ea quae sunt ultima res sacramenti excedit baptismus sanguinis, quia et gratia in baptismo sanguinis magis augetur habenti, et amplior datur non habenti, si impedimentum non adsit; et remissio peccatorum quamvis non sit plenior, quia uterque omnem poenam et culpam tollit, tamen est in baptismo sanguinis efficacior et fructuosior, quia secundis maculis non inquinatur.*

The Baptism of water conforms to him by sacramental signification, but the Baptism of blood in all reality. Accordingly, Baptism of water enjoys pre-eminence in respect of the sacramental sign, as in the impression of the character and the like. But Baptism of blood enjoys pre-eminence in respect of those things that are the ultimate point of the sacrament. For in the Baptism of blood grace is the more increased for one who has grace and (if there be no impediment) more fully given to the one who has not. And though the remission of sins is not fuller, since it takes away both every penalty and every fault, nonetheless it is in the Baptism of blood more efficacious and fruitful, because not spoiled by subsequent stains.

The trinitarian economy in the light of which *Gaudium et Spes* 22 sees the salvific work of God beyond the bounds of the visible sacraments is found very explicitly in St Thomas' treatment of the Baptism of blood in the *Summa Theologiae* III, q. 66, arts. 11–12. The work of *consociatio* to the Paschal Mystery is primarily that of the Holy Spirit, and so exceeds the order of visible signs:

Baptismus aquae efficaciam habet a passione Christi cui aliquis configuratur per baptismum; et ulterius sicut a prima causa, a Spiritu Sancto. Licet autem effectus dependeat a prima causa, causa tamen superexcedit effectum, nec dependet ab effectu. Et ideo praeter baptismum aquae, potest aliquis consequi sacramenti effectum ex passione Christ, inquantum quis ei conformatur pro Christo patiendo.[6]

The baptism of water draws its efficacy from the Passion of Christ to whom a person is conformed by Baptism, and more ultimately, as from its first cause, from the Holy Spirit. It may be, however, that the effect will depend on that first cause, the cause far exceeding the effect and not depending on it. Over and above the Baptism of water, therefore, someone may gain the effect of the sacrament from the Passion of Christ, inasmuch as they are conformed to the suffering Christ.

virtus Spiritus Sancti operatur . . . in baptismo sanguinis per potissimum dilectionis et affectionis fervorem . . . Baptismus sanguinis praeminentiam habet non solum ex parte passionis Christi, sed etiam ex parte Spiritus Sancti ut dictum est.[7]

. . . the power of the Holy Spirit works . . . in the Baptism of blood through more powerful love and affection . . . The Baptism of blood has its pre-eminence not only from the side of Christ but also from that of the Holy Spirit, as has been said above.

It might be objected that none of these passages refers to children before the age of reason, and that the Baptism of blood implies a martyrdom consciously undergone. We must concede that none of the passages wherein the Fathers speak of the Baptism of blood explicitly mention infants, yet in answer it must be pointed out that the *ratio* for the Baptism of blood is never given as anything but the objective conformity to Christ's death, not the subjective exercise of virtue in martyrdom.

As for St Thomas, it is true that he never explicitly speaks of the Baptism of blood in the case of infants,[8] yet in his tract on the sacrament of Penance in the *Summa Theologiae* he goes so far as to say that a *sleeping* man, already baptized, who is in the state of *mortal* sin and who is killed for the sake of Christ will have his sins forgiven, as long as there is not at that moment an actual will to sin, since *passio pro Christo suscepta obtinet vim baptismi*: 'suffering unto death undergone on account of Christ obtains the power of Baptism.'[9] *A fortiori*, then, St Thomas would accept the Baptism of blood for the remission of *original* sin in unconscious infants.[10]

Commentators, however, like Cajetan and Billuart[11] and Thomistic theologians like Prümmer and Journet explicitly teach the efficacy of Baptism of blood for infants.[12] Unlike the Baptism of desire, which is of a subjective, moral nature working *ex opere operantis*, the Baptism of blood is a physical, objective conformity to the passion, and so works for the remission of sin and the bestowal of grace *ex opere operato*, as water Baptism. Journet sums up their teaching thus:

> Unbaptised infants who – still today – are killed in hatred of Christ or of the Christian religion, are martyrs. If enquiry into the circumstances of their deaths led to certainty that there were killed out of hatred for Christ, the Church could canonise them and celebrate them by a feast day, as she does, on 28 December, the martyrdom of the Holy Innocents.[13]

The precision made by Journet 'if enquiry into the circumstances of their death led to certainty', leads us to the next point regarding the case of infants who die by abortion. Granted that justification by Baptism of blood is possible for the unborn, can this manner of *consociatio* be attributed to all or only some of them? In other words is their death always brought about *in odium fidei*? This could only be established by a reliable inductive study of individual cases. It would appear that some person who shared formal imputability for the abortion would have to be formally motivated by hatred for the truths of the Catholic faith or the virtues of the Christian life. Cases *super martyrio* in the Congregation of the Causes of Saints, following the authoritative treatment of martyrdom in Benedict XIV's *De Servorum Dei Beatificatione et Beatorum Canonizatione*,[14] require proof not only on the part of the martyr, but also *ex parte tyrannidis* ('on the part of the tyrant'), of his intention to kill out of hatred for the faith and life of Christians.

That many such cases exist among the millions of abortions that occur is more than likely. Yet some abortions may be committed in good faith, and, if we accept the principles of Catholic morality, might even be subjectively good or even virtuous acts, if the agent of the deed is invincibly ignorant. Such cases probably multiply with the diffusion of a culture which does not teach the malice of abortion. St Thomas teaches, after all, that it is possible to be invincibly ignorant even of the more evident conclusions of the natural law.[15] Furthermore, some women may be motivated to have an abortion by the thought that the child will go to Heaven and so avoid the miseries of earthly life. Such a mother is thus motivated by a love for the truths of faith, however tragically misguided and mistaken her application of them may be. Others – and these are in all likelihood the greater number – are motivated by pure convenience and never give the faith a thought in their considerations. Such abortions as are described here could not possibly be martyrdoms.[16]

There is another fact, more profound than the question of the circumstances which would define martyrdom, which makes it impossible to characterize all the unborn killed by abortion as martyrs: *There is no physical certainty about the precise point of the infusion of the spiritual, rational soul.* This is a strictly philosophical question, which the Magisterium of the Church has repeatedly stated it is not competent, or at least declines to determine. The grave immorality of abortion remains in any case absolutely certain, and so the embryo or fetus must be treated as a person, yet the bodily disposition necessary for the infusion of the soul is a matter for philosophical debate, taking into account the evidence, always inconclusive in itself, of embryology. This teaching, which has been carefully nuanced, repeated, and referenced in the Holy Office's 1987 *Instructio* (I, 1) and in Pope John Paul II's 1995 *Evangelium Vitae* (60) was presented in the Holy See's *Declaratio de abortu procurato* of 1974 thus:

Haec declaratio consulto quaestionem reliquam facit, quo temporis memento anima spiritualis infundatur. Qua de re ut traditio non est unanima, ita auctores inter se differunt. Nam cum alii affirment id primo vitae tempore fieri, aliis placet non hoc ante fieri quam germen in sua sede steterit. Nimirum non est scientiae dirimere quaestiones, quia existentia animae immortalis ad eiusdem provincia non pertinet. Agitur enim de quaestione philosophiae propria, a qua haec moralis affirmatio nullo modo dependet, duabus de his causis: 1) quia, etiam si ponatur infusionem animae tardius supervenire, est nihilominus in fetu incipiens humana vita (de qua biologicae scientiae ope constat), quae et praeparat et exigit animam, per quam natura a parentibus accepta perficiatur; 2) quia si modo tamquam probabilis illa animae infusio, de qua dicimus (non enim de re contraria umquam constabit), iudicetur, vitam ei adimere idem est ac periculo se committere occidendi hominis, non tamquam in spe, sed omnino anima instructi.[17]

This Declaration expressly leaves aside the question of the moment when the spiritual soul is infused. There is not a unanimous tradition on this point and authors are as yet in disagreement. For some it dates from the first instant, for others it could not at least precede nidation. It is not within the competence of science to decide between these views, because the existence of an immortal soul is not a question in its field. It is a philosophical problem from which our moral affirmation remains independent for two reasons: (i) supposing a later animation, there is still nothing less than a *human* life, preparing for and calling for soul in which the nature received from the parents is perfected; (ii) on the other hand it suffices that this presence of the soul be probable (and one can never prove the contrary) in order that the taking of life involve accepting the risk of killing a man, not only waiting for, but already in possession of his soul.

If any verifiable cases of an abortion undertaken *in odium fidei* could be found, then they would need to have been at such a stage of gestation at which no integrally Catholic philosopher or theologian would question the presence of a rational soul. Perhaps this would be after the first trimester, but in any case the *status quaestionis*, one which the Magisterium has called *properly* philosophical, would rule out the possibility that even every abortion performed *in odium fidei* could be said to be a martyrdom.

III. The current theological context of the discussion of possible modes of justification for infants who die before Baptism.

Now we can answer our question: *Is there a possible mode of accomplishing a 'consociatio' to the Lord's death proper to the experience of those killed in their mothers' wombs, or does this differ accidentally among them?* There is no mode of accomplishing a *consociatio* to the Lord's death proper to their experience, because not all of the unborn die for the same reason. Some, it is practically certain, die as martyrs, and for them the realization of the doctrine of *Gaudium et Spes* is clear, amply and unanimously accounted for in patristic, Thomistic, and contemporary theology. Some, probably the majority, die for other reasons, and for these theology seeks to understand in the light of Tradition how the Holy Spirit offers to them the possibility of a *consociatio* to the Paschal Mystery. Others may never had had a concretely personal existence at all, and so they are not among those for whom the *vocatio hominis* of which *Gaudium et Spes* 22 speaks continues after death.

As was indicated above, we now pass to a more general consideration of the possibility of a *consociatio* to the Paschal Mystery on the part of infants who die before baptism, whether in the womb or not, by procured abortion or otherwise, excluding only the case already expounded of infants killed *in odium fidei*, for whom the manner of *consociatio*, as we have seen, is Baptism of blood. Although the treatment of this issue is not required by the question at hand, it is strongly suggested by it, especially as it seems that the response to the *dubium expositum* will be, after all, *negative*, albeit with important qualifications. And so, in order to complement and complete the points already made, especially insofar as a deeper consideration of the perspective of *Gaudium et Spes* 22 can be obtained, we will consider the case of infants dying before baptism generally.

First of all, it is necessary to make some broad observations about the question of the state of merely natural happiness commonly called the Limbo of Children: *limbus puerorum*. The current tendency to reject the once universal common teaching of theologians on the *limbus puerorum* and the concrete possibility of a state of merely natural happiness is the result of the rejection by contemporary theology of the possibility of a state of pure nature. The rejection of this latter doctrine is founded on a more fundamental reluctance to distinguish in the historical concrete between the natural and supernatural orders.

Now the speculative question of the distinction and relation between the two orders of nature and grace is an extremely difficult one which requires a keen sense of the analogical use of terms. The opposition natural-supernatural is particularly polyvalent, especially in St Thomas, and cannot be reduced to one situation among many analogous ones, e.g. to the movement of a natural potency to act. The affirmations of St Thomas (who never spoke of a *status naturae purae*, a 'state of pure nature') about a natural *desire* for the vision of the divine essence which utterly exceeds the *powers* of nature are the clearest vindication of this point. The classical commentators' reduction of this natural desire to the merest obediential potency and non-repugnance of nature or to an elicited *personal* desire, when St Thomas calls it a *natural* one, is an evidently inadequate and even theologically disastrous solution. Not only is St Thomas's thought in all its formal rigour rendered needlessly unintelligible, but grace is made radically extrinsic, and possibly irrelevant, to nature. If this was the mind set which allowed for a purely natural happiness, then it is not surprising that contemporary theologians have been suspicious of the notion.

On the other hand, the rejection of these theories must not lead to the opposite error, namely, that of making a supernatural end a concrete exigency of nature. This was the error condemned in *Humani Generis*, the intention of which condemnation was clear enough: the vindication of the gratuity of grace (not at all a redundant expression in the light of contemporary neo-Pelagianism), even if its formulation may have been hampered by the retention of the perspective of the commentators.

What to do with a merely natural happiness and the *limbus puerorum?* To assert its reality seems to many to fall into a kind of rationalistic and abstract account of human nature incompatible with the concrete historical fact of human nature assumed and redeemed by God the incarnate Word. More on this later. To deny it means, quite simply, to assert that there is concretely a way whereby all infants who die without water Baptism can have original sin remitted. Let us take a look a how this might come about.

IV Possible modes of justification other than Baptism of blood for infants who die before Baptism

The most reasonable explanation of how an infant who dies before Baptism could be justified without the Baptism of blood is by a Baptism of desire made possible by an interior illumination either directly from God or through an angel. Such knowledge would be infused into the soul of the child as would make him capable, under the movement of grace, to elicit the act of desire for Baptism, the *baptismus flaminis*, which would obtain his justification. This kind of *consociatio* by Baptism of desire as regards its mode of operation is more remote from Christ's Passion as cause of justification than water Baptism, and more remote still from the real identification with the Passion found in the Baptism of blood, but it is, according to the whole of Tradition, including even St Augustine, an efficacious replacement when neither of the other are possible. We will not, however, examine the *monumenta*, the monuments of theological tradition for this type of Baptism as we did for the Baptism of blood, since it is not directly needed for the question at hand, but will take it for granted. Baptism of desire requires a conscious choice, and so works *ex opere operantis*, unlike sacramental and martyric Baptism which work their effects *ex opere operato*.

That such a thing is possible cannot be doubted.[18] Even so, there is no way to know with any certainty if such a manner of *consociatio* in fact takes place, and if so, under what conditions. To assert that such a means is universally available is only to offer an opinion about a possibility which has a degree of probability impossible to determine. There are simply no monuments of Tradition or of the Magisterium which would lead us to any more definite knowledge than this.

There is another opinion, widely held today, originating with Cajetan, that it is the faith of the child's parents, or of the Church which obtains the grace of justification. Since, however, this desire is a kind of impetration for the infant, it would operate as a moral cause *ex opere operantis*, from the activity of the agent and would thus have to be explained as obtaining the grace of an interior illumination for him which would enable him to elicit an act of desire for Baptism. It thus is reduced to the case of Baptism of desire through interior illumination. It simply cannot be that the desire of the parents is more efficacious than the *baptismus flaminis* itself, yet such would be the case if it were interpreted as having any more efficacy than that of prayer for the child. For if the faith or desire or intention of the parents or of anyone else were to operate directly and of itself to justify the infant as a physical cause, then the expression of this desire would not be so much of *votum* or prayer for the child, as it would be rather some kind of sacrament different from water Baptism or its equivalents, configuring him to Christ's Passion.[19]

Of this there can be no question, as there are only seven sacraments instituted by Christ, and he has reserved their institution to himself, not sharing it with any other.[20]

The solution of interior illumination which makes possible a Baptism of desire poses another problem: if this illumination is given to all the infants who are not able to be baptized before their death, then this would also include the possibility that certain ones could be tempted and then freely reject the graces given, and commit a grave sin and so be eternally lost. So this theory creates a possibility far more unpleasant to contemplate than that of a permanent state of natural happiness! Yet there is no reason to assert that the *liberum arbitrium*, free will, which characterizes all other human choices short of the beatific vision would be lacking in this case. If one considers the demonic agency at work to some extent in every abortion, then would it not be possible for the infant to be tempted to a hatred for his persecutors, or to sin against the fourth commandment by despising his parents? An abortion could then include a dreadful moral drama for the infant, possibly well beyond the horror of the outrage to his rights as a person.

From the preceding discussion it is evident why the Magisterium of the Church teaches that the thought of God's mercy will merely '*allow* us to hope that there is a way of salvation for children who have died without Baptism.' And that the uncertainty renders 'all the more urgent' the call to baptize infants. And this because 'the Church does not know of any means other than Baptism that ensures entry into eternal beatitude', even as she recognizes the efficacy of the Baptisms of blood and of desire.[21] Nothing certain, but only possibilities, or at most some probabilities, can be discovered regarding the justification of infants who die before Baptism without being martyred. This is the teaching of the Church, as well as of theological reasoning.

Now if we are unable, even with the help of the Church's Tradition and Magisterium, to rise beyond a certain level of theological opinion regarding the justification of infants who die before Baptism without the Baptism of blood, then this requires us to consider the possibility that these infants do not obtain the remission of original sin at all. How could this square with *Gaudium et Spes* 22 which clearly teaches that *all* have the possibility offered them of a *consociatio* with the Paschal Mystery? The answer to this question is not as difficult to find as one might think.

V. Florence and Vatican II: A *consociatio* to the Paschal Mystery for infants who die before water Baptism without undergoing a Baptism of blood based on absolute certainties.

It is *de fide definita* – a matter of defined faith – from the Bull *Laetentur Caeli* of the Council of Florence that those who die with unremitted original sin go immediately into Hell, to receive a punishment, however, that differs from those who are condemned for personal mortal sin:

> *Diffinimus ... illorum animas qui in actuali mortali peccato vel solo originali decedunt, mox in infernum descendere, poenis tamen disparibus puniendas.*[22]

> We define ... that the souls of those who die in actual mortal sin or simply in original sin go down shortly to Hell, to undergo, however, penalties of unequal sorts.

Such a definition requires a Catholic to profess at least the possibility of such a case. Of course, it seems unreasonable that the Church would define dogmatically a mere possibility. Yet this dogmatically certain possibility has to be squared with what is a similarly solemn declaration of the Second Vatican Council, whose solemnity is expressed in the words *tenere debemus* found in *Gaudium et Spes* 22, that there is a real possibility offered to each human person of a share in the Paschal Mystery of Christ.

Now we shall see precisely how the historical, incarnational perspective of the Council can shed precious light on the question of the fate of infants who die without the remission of original sin. It should be noted that the assertion of *Gaudium et Spes* that Christ is in some way united with each human person by reason of his Incarnation, and that all men are afforded the concrete possibility *ut paschali mysterio consocientur* nowhere speaks of salvation in that perfect sense which includes the possession of the beatific vision. Could it be that the *vocatio hominis* which is *revera una et divina* of which the Council speaks does not mean only the possession of supernatural beatitude, but rather the individual and collective *consociatio* of all men to Christ as the New Adam and the Head of the human race? Might this include other means of *consociatio* other than the most perfect one?

Christ's work offers the human race freedom from sin and death in the resurrected life of a restored humanity. The persons who are in a condition of natural happiness in the *limbus puerorum* have been freed from sin, for they have paid the debt of original sin by undergoing the punishment of bodily death. Being innocent of all personal sin, they do not suffer the consequences of it, nor do they suffer from the disturbances of concupiscence. What is more, by the efficacy of Christ's own Resurrection they will rise from the dead in the full perfection of their age and natural beauty. This is a work of divine, not human power.

It is precisely the resurrection which establishes their *consociatio* with Christ. Their resurrection is his work whereby they can be included in a single redeemed human race, restored in the specific, bodily unity it lost in the Fall and marred by further sin. True, they lack the perfect fullness of supernatural beatitude, but they possess the fullness of human natural life and integrity, individual and social, because of their organic union with Christ in his Incarnation and Resurrection. In them he has also triumphed over sin and death. It cannot be denied that this is a true *consociatio* to the Paschal Mystery. Let us hear Cardinal Journet:

> The children in limbo died before the time when one awakes here below to the realities of grace and sin, Christ and Belial. They escape the alternative of Heaven and Hell; they remain always on this side of the river. But they do not escape the universal saving plan. It is to the Christ who took on our human nature to rehabilitate it in all those who pose no obstacle thereto that they owe from the moment of their deaths their entry into the felicity of Limbo. It is to Christ that at the end of time they will owe the resurrection of their bodies, no longer feeble and fragile but adapted to the full deployment of their natural life of knowledge and love. They are gathered around Christ and conformed to him inasmuch as he is become, by the redemptive Incarnation, the Head and repairer of humanity.[23]

The 'incarnational' perspective on Limbo has the great merit of simplicity in the application of principles known to be absolutely certain. It is sure that all are included in God's salvific will. It is certain that the Church knows of no means for the salvation of infants other than Baptism or its equivalent. It is a defined dogma that those who die in original sin are deprived of the supernatural vision of God. It is sure that all will rise by the efficacy of Christ's Resurrection. It is certain that no one is punished personally except for personal sin. Whatever can be said about the *limbus puerorum*, it cannot be said that it is based on merely speculative probabilities. Rather, it is a conclusion drawn from the dogmatic certainties.

Other theories which try to establish a justification of infants without Baptism of water or of blood deal in mere moral possibilities, and cannot conclude with any certainty. The doctrine of Limbo avoids a multiplicity of *theologumena* based on possibilities which the zeal of the theologian for his opinion might tempt him to force into some note or other of doctrinal certainty by over-interpreting recent magisterial texts, and over-extending the assertions of classical authorities meant only to refer to exceptional cases. Cardinal Journet speaks wisely and convincingly of the danger of a mistaken theological method which abuses mere possibilities or probabilities:

> We have set out, you see, from what is certain to climb up into the regions of what is probable. That is the method of the ancients, and it is the only safe method. It leads to postulating, not evacuating, the mystery of Limbo. To want to invert that method is a grave error whose present-day victims are only too numerous. People set out from the conjectural conclusions of their predecessors and by a contrary route, proceeding up the road they came down, finish by calling into question that which was certain.
>
> The salutary efficacy of the initiation sacrament of the law of nature is regarded as certain, whereas the ancients affirmed this only for the epoch before Christ when the law of the Gospel had not been promulgated. This sacrament is declared valid even where the law of Christ is promulgated in such a way that it forms a doublet of Baptism and evacuates the latter's absolute necessity. The efficacy of this sacrament of nature is extended to infants still enclosed in their mother's womb, something the ancients never did. People go still further, assuring us that the justifying faith of an adult or of the Church can, by directing the appropriate intention, be in some way transferred to the child. They encourage in the faithful a *lex orandi* which will become one day, it is hoped, a *lex credendi*. Either partially or completely the mystery of Limbo is pushed to one side. And it is in virtue of these results that they undertake to revise the constant teachings of the Magisterium and to reinterpret the initial biblical revelation.[24]

The doctrine of Limbo also sheds light on the broader meaning of human salvation and vocation in Christ, not taking opposition of nature and super-nature as the exclusive context of the question of human salvation, but rather seeing even this opposition in the light of the concrete, historical, even physical order of the Incarnation, and the variety of conditions that follow from it. This approach leaves intact the gratuity of a grace not due to nature, while maintaining the supreme natural appropriateness for a rational nature capable on its own of knowing God by analogy of a beatitude which consists of a vision of the divine nature. It does not assert that a merely natural happiness is anything more than the *poena mitissima*, 'the gentlest punishment', to use St Augustine's expression, for original sin, and does not conceive of it as the expression of some possible (or futurible!) *status naturae purae* apart from the order of the redemption wrought by Christ. It involves a properly divine work which is at the threshold of the strictly supernatural, a miracle, namely, the bodily resurrection, the result of which is nonetheless a natural bodily life. None of the important speculative questions regarding nature and super-nature are abused or minimized, but they are put in their place within the wider context of the Incarnation of the Head of human nature.

Furthermore the doctrine of Limbo accommodates better the Eastern theological tradition, which has always emphasized the variety of conditions experienced in the life to come without fixing on the vision of the divine essence as the unique form of eternal happiness for man. The question of the salvation of the unbaptized infants is mostly a Latin anxiety, born from a perspective which emphasizes almost exclusively the beatific vision and the gratuity of grace, and often minimizes other aspects of man's perfection which are more evident in the Eastern tradition, such as the restoration of the life of Eden and the bodily resurrection as the definitive moment of human salvation, before which no one enters into beatitude in the fullest sense. St Gregory Nazianzen says that the unbaptized child is 'neither glorified nor punished' after death, since he lacks the grace of Baptism, but has never sinned, a simple description of Limbo.[25] St Gregory of Nyssa grants the infants a true knowledge of God, but one which is completely natural and proportionate to their lack of personal merits.[26]

The Greek Fathers explain the differences in the levels of knowledge of God by the diversity of merits of the souls of the departed, rather than on their possession of supernatural or natural life, as the Latin tradition does. It is not difficult to see that the Latin and Greek traditions are broadly complementary. The merits of men are, after all, qualified by their possession of natural or supernatural life. Whereas the Latin tradition sees the differences as parallel orders of life and operation, the Greek sees them as a contained in a continuum open to progress and development up to the final judgement and resurrection.

VI. Some responses to objections to the doctrine of a purely natural happiness for infants who die without Baptism or martyrdom.

The objection could be raised that the deprivation of the beatific vision, the *poena damni*, to which the persons in Limbo are subjected on account of their dying in the state of original sin (a possibility which, it is good to recall again, is a defined dogma) is the *greatest* of the punishments of the lost, and so seems particularly severe for those who have no personal fault. St Thomas answers this objection as follows in the *De Malo* q.5, a.1, ad 3.:

> ... *Gravitas alicuius poenae potest attendi dupliciter. Uno modo ex parte ipsius boni quod privatur per malum poenae; et sic carentia visionis divinae et fruitionis Dei, est gravissima poenarum. Alio modo per comparationem ad eum qui punitur; et sic tanto est gravior poena, quanto id quod subtrahitur est magis proprium et connaturale ei cui subtrahitur; sicut magis diceremus puniri hominem si auferretur ei patrimonium suum, quam si impediretur ne perveniret ad regnum quod ei non debetur. Et per hunc modum dicitur esse mitissima omnium poenarum sola carentia visionis divinae essentiae est quoddam bonum omnino supernaturale.*[27]

The gravity of some penalty can be considered in two ways. One way is from the side of that good of which the ill that is penalty deprives one. And in that sense the lack of divine vision and the enjoyment of God is the gravest of penalties. But another way of looking at this is by comparing the penalty to the one penalised. And here the gravity of the penalty is greater in dependence on the degree to which what is taken from the one penalised is the more proper and connatural to him. We say, after all, that a man has been punished more heavily if his patrimony is removed from him than if he is prevented from inheriting a throne to which he had no right. And in this sense the sole lack of the vision of the divine essence is the lightest of all penalties being as it is a good of an altogether supernatural kind.

Another objection might be raised based on the recent affirmation of Pope John Paul II in *Evangelium Vitae*, 99 that the children killed in abortion are alive in the Lord and that their mothers will be able to ask forgiveness of them. How is this compatible with possibility defined by the Council of Florence and expressed in the doctrine

of Limbo that they are separated from God in hell? St Thomas in
In II Sent. dist. 30, q.2, a.2, ad 5, again answers the objection:

> *Quamvis pueri non baptizati sint separati a Deo, quantum ad illam
> coniunctionem quae est per gloriam, non tamen ab eo penitus separati
> sunt. Imo ipsi coniunguntur per participationem naturalium
> bonorum; et ita etiam de ipso gaudere poterunt naturali cognitione et
> dilectione.*

Though unbaptized infants are separated from God with
respect to that conjoining that is through glory, they are not
penally separated from him. They are very closely conjoined
with him through their participation in natural goods; and
thus they will be able to rejoice in him by natural knowledge
and love.

Living in the Lord does not require a supernatural knowledge and
love of him, nor does a merely natural condition rule out prayer
for or communication with their parents. This communication
seems to be even more likely after the general resurrection.

The most general objection to the doctrine of Limbo is that it
seems to be derogatory of divine Providence. What is the good,
redounding to God's glory, that could be drawn from the condition of the persons in Limbo? How, in particular is his justice
vindicated, since they are deprived through no fault of their own?

St Gregory of Nyssa explains the premature death of infants as a
particular disposition of God's Providence preventing them from
grave sins which he foresees they will commit if they live. A more
formally profound version of this insight was offered by the anti-
Jansenist Benedictine Cardinal Celestine Sfrondrati in the
seventeenth century. He taught that the personal innocence and
utter freedom from sin and concupiscence are, under a certain
objective aspect, superior to the gift of grace itself: *beneficium longe
praestantius quam gratia sufficiens.* Never to have offended God in
the slightest degree is a blessing so great that the persons in Limbo
would rather be deprived of the chance of Heaven, than to have
offended God. The inhabitants of Limbo are then witnesses to a
hatred of sin and to a love of God which places his honour above
their own proper good.[28] They thus share a personal quality with
Our Lord, his Mother, possibly St Joseph and St John the Baptist,
and the child martyrs, showing to all the elect that this perfect
personal innocence is the gift of the very least of Christ's brethren.

Yet this is a vindication only of the specific Providence of God with regard to the persons in Limbo as individuals. There is another, more general aspect of this Providence which is illustrated by the existence of an everlasting state of natural happiness. Christ as the New Adam is not only the supernatural, but also the natural Head of the human race. As Head and King of our race he has a human nature with all its natural qualities and limitations. He restores this nature in every human person, in some by its glorification by grace, in others in its natural perfection, but in all by the power of his resurrection to an immortal life.[29] The doctrine of a purely natural happiness in a resurrected humanity for those who die *cum solo originali* glorifies the order and perfection of divine providence. It reveals the universal salvific will of God in Christ, in whom God gives to each one all the riches of nature and grace which his individual capacity can receive according to his experiences in the body. It is a true *consociatio* to the Paschal Mystery, a limited, but real salvation for human nature disrupted by the Fall and its consequences. In this light we can appreciate the edifying exclamation of Cardinal Journet:

> O little children who died without baptism, reproved ones who have never done evil, you are not an accident in the divine economy, a peculiar case that busy, distracted theologians manage as best they can, an insignificant parenthesis. Your role is great, and your destiny well determined, highly significant. You are the first-fruits of natural felicity, of nature divinely restored.[30]

VII. A practical suggestion in the light of the answer to the question: 'Can the Magisterium of the Church acknowledge children killed in abortion as "Companions of the Holy Innocents" (and therefore martyrs)?'

The answer given here to the question at hand is thus a qualified 'no'. Here are the qualifications on the practical level. There is nothing to hinder and everything to encourage an association of the faithful to seek out reliable testimony of cases of infants aborted *in odium fidei*. With this knowledge a cause could be initiated with the *nihil obstat* of the Congregation of the Causes of Saints on the local level. This could lead to the beatification of one or more of these children, as many as can be proven to be martyrs. They should be given names, perhaps by their repentant parents, if these are living and desire to participate in the cause. The edification to the faithful of 'Child martyrs' of abortion would be considerable and the graces of intercession could be with confidence invoked on the world. Other cases could be added later by way of a simple aggregation with a decree *super martyrio* and equivalent beatification. Canonization would follow after an examination of the pastoral benefits (conversions, miracles of intercession, etc.) of the beatification, and thus the whole Catholic world could rejoice in their earthly glorification. The text of the introit for their Roman rite memorial could be taken from *IV Esdras*, which apocryphal book the Church uses for her other largely 'forgotten' holy ones, the souls in Purgatory, in the introit *Requiem aeternam*:

Iucundare mater, cum filiis tuis, quia ego te eripiam dicit Dominus. Filios tuos dormientes memorare, quoniam ego eos educam e lateribus terrae, et misericordiam cum illis faciam, quoniam misericors sum, dicit Dominus omnipotens. Amplectere natos tuos usque dum venio, et praestem illis misericordiam, quoniam exubuerant fontes mei, et gratia mea non deficiet.[31]

Be joyful, mother, you and your sons, for I will come to your rescue. Remember your children who sleep in the grave; I will bring them up from the depths of the earth, and show mercy to them; for I am merciful, says the Lord almighty. Cherish your children until I come, and proclaim my mercy to them; for my favour flows abundantly from springs that will never run dry.

Notes

[1] *Gaudium et Spes*, no. 22.

[2] There are affirmations of St Augustine in this line as well that enter the Latin scholastic tradition mostly through Julian of Toledo's *Prognosticon futuri saeculi*; however, we are using only the Greek Fathers here since they have more explicitly given the *ratio* of the Baptism of blood as a *real* identification with the Passion of the Lord.

[3] Origen has six, Damascene eight, and St Thomas attributes to Damascene nine, but all the divisions include at least the five given by Gregory Nazianzen.

[4] *Theological Discourse* 39, 17 in the *Sources Chrétiennes* edition vol. 358.

[5] *Oratio Catechetica*, 35, PG Vol. 45, col. 90.

[6] a.11, corpus.

[7] a.12, corpus and ad 3.

[8] St Thomas does hold that the Holy Innocents were true martyrs, albeit *imperfecta ratione*, but this is not for him the cause of their initial justification, at least for the majority of them, since they were circumcised.

9 S. Th. III, q. 87, a.1, ad 2.

10 St Bonaventure, it should be noted, quite explicitly rejects Baptism of blood for infants, except in the extremely limited and improbable case of a child killed *on the way to be baptized* and *in order that he not be baptized. In IV Sent.* dist. IV, p. II, dubium 4. He is generally less willing to grant the preeminence of the Baptism of blood to water Baptism, although he does hold that it is superior *simpliciter.* For example, he does not accept that Baptism of blood can justify someone in the state of mortal sin without at least attrition, whereas St Thomas holds that it justifies so long as there is no rejection of the grace of martyrdom, or sinful act at the moment of martyrdom.

11 *Tractatus de Fortitudine* diss. I, art. 2, *'De Martyrio': Sunt ergo Ss. Innocentes dicendi martyres martyrio sumpto non pro voluntaria mortis acceptatione propter Christum, sed pro ipsa morte propter Christum tollerata; quomodo etiam nunc forent martyres infantes nondum baptizati, qui in odium Christi aut religionis Christianae occiderentur.* 'The Holy Innocents are thus to be called martyrs since they underwent martyrdom not by way of a voluntary acceptance of death for Christ, but by way of their very death undergone on his account; and in this sense there can still be infants as yet unbaptized who are martyrs, being slain in hatred for Christ or the Christian religion.'

12 The Thomistic moral theologian Dominic Prümmer, O.P. in his *Theologia Moralis* v.II, p. 624 is one of the few who mentions the case of the unborn *explicitly: ... ex doctrina fere communi theologorum non tantum Innocentes occisi ab Herode, sed quicumque parvuli necati pro christiana fide (etiam qui in utero matris occiduntur) sunt martyres et vitam aeternam obtinebunt.* '... from the common doctrine of theologians not just the Innocents killed by Herod but all infants whatsoever slain for the Christian faith (even in their mother's womb) are martyrs and will obtain eternal life.'

13 Charles Journet, *La Volonté divine salvifique sur les petits enfants,* (Paris: Desclée de Brouwer, 1959), p. 79.

14 *Liber* III, cc.11–13.

15 S. Th. I–II q. 94, a.6.

16 The malice of remote causes is not sufficient to establish martyrdom: this is clear from the teaching of Benedict XIV in the treatise cited. The great canonist teaches that the persecutor must intervene directly in the martyrdom. Thus the *odium fidei* of the demons inciting a man to procure an abortion could not justify the note of martyrdom, unless the man who directly causes the abortion is also so motivated, or is only an instrumental, not a morally imputable cause of the death, a case which would require some form of possession. If the fallen Angels' hatred of the faith were used generally to qualify the abortion as a martyrdom, then every murder, indeed every death, if we take into account the words of the Book of Wisdom about the envy of the devil, could be called a martyrdom. Only if the death occurred by direct demonic intervention could the one killed be said to have been

martyred by demonic malice. The only certain cases we know of murders committed by a demon are those of Asmodaeus in the Book of Tobit. If such a case exists in the case of an unborn child, and perhaps it does, it would be practically impossible to prove. It requires either the *reliable* testimony of the possessed, or a true miracle to attest the fact of an invisible demonic intervention without the aid of a human instrument.

[17] Congregatio pro Doctrina Fidei, *Declaratio de abortu procurato*, no. 16.

[18] The certainty of the possibility of such an illumination is established by the reasoning of such passages of St Thomas as *De Veritate*, q. 14, a.11, ad 1: ... *ad divinum providentiam pertinet ut cuilibet provideat de necessariis ad salutem, dummodo ex parte eius non impediatur. Si enim aliquis taliter nutritus (viz 'in silvis vel inter bruta animalia'), ductum ratio-nis naturalis sequeretur in appetitu boni et fuga mali, certissime est tenendum, quos Deus ei vel per internam inspirationem revelaret ea quae sunt necessaria ad credendum, vel aliquem fidei praedicatorem ad eum dirigeret, sicut misit Petrum ad Cornelium.* 'It belongs to divine providence to furnish any person whatever with the necessary means of salvation, provided this is not impeded from the side of the subject. For if someone thus nurtured (viz. in the woods, or among brute animals) by the guidance of natural reason follows in his appetites the good and flees the evil, it must be held most assuredly that God will reveal to him by internal inspiration those things that must necessarily be believed, or direct some preacher of the faith to him as he sent Peter to Cornelius.' Such a passage does not, however, apply precisely to infants before the use of reason, but the *ratio* used, that of divine Providence, is illuminating and challenging, as will be seen later on.

[19] In reply to the objection that some expression of the desire of the parents could function for the child in the way that rites inspired by the natural law did for Gentiles, and circumcision did for the Jews before the promulgation of the New Law, it must be answered that such rites were efficacious insofar as they *prefigured* Christian Baptism, and expressed the desire of the parents for the fulfilment of the prefiguration. It is not possible to say with any certainty that such rites still have a moral efficacy now, after the institution of the sacrament of Baptism. Cf. S. Th. III, q. 70, a.4, ad 2.

[20] Cf. S. Th. III, q. 64, a.4.

[21] CCC, nos. 1257–1261.

[22] Concilium Florentinum, Bulla *Laetentur Caeli*, 6 iul. 1439: DH, 1306. The text was taken almost verbatim from the profession of faith required of the Emperor Michael Palaeologus at the Second Council of Lyons in 1274.

[23] C. Journet, *La Volonté divine*, op. cit., 40.

[24] Ibid., 131. This is an almost scathingly accurate description of the exploitation of St Thomas and the Fathers by a kind of casuistry applied to authoritative *loci theologici*. We have even heard a professor at a Roman athenaeum insist that one may no longer reasonably hold

the doctrine of Limbo since the new *Catechism* does not mention it!
Apart from the observation which could be made that the old, but still
authoritative *Catechism of the Council of Trent* did not mention Limbo
either, such 'magisterial positivism' is not serious theology, no matter
how 'orthodox' its practitioners.

25 *Theological Orations*, 40, 23, in the *Sources Chrétiennes* edition, vol. 358.

26 *Ad Hierum, de Infantibus qui praemature abripiuntur*, PG Vol. 46, col. 178:
In this treatise, Gregory of Nyssa does not see the problem so much as
the lack of baptismal grace, as of the absence of personal merits. In
any case, it is clear that Gregory of Nyssa's treatment of the knowledge
of God and happiness proper to infants is purely based upon the principles of philosophical anthropology and theodicy, with almost no
reference to the mysteries of faith. His approach is more formally
naturalistic than any of the baroque Thomistic commentators with
their *status naturae purae*! Of course, this may be ascribed to the
exceedingly concrete approach of the Origenistic tradition which
does not so much deny the distinction of nature and super-nature in
Man as it ignores it.

27 Note here that St Thomas interprets the notorious *poena mitissima* of
St Augustine, as being precisely the lack of the beatific vision, and the
possession of the fullness of natural contemplation possible to Man
without supernatural aid.

28 Cardinal Celestine Sfondrati, OSB, *Nodus praedestinationis dissolutus*,
(Rome, 1687), pp. 120, 164.

29 Even the damned *in actuali mortali peccato* (to use the words of the
Council of Florence) would receive a risen body caused by the resurrection of Christ (albeit as efficient and not exemplary cause) which
has all the natural perfections of the risen bodies of the blessed and
the persons in Limbo. St Thomas in the Commentary on the
Sentences, and in the *résumé* of his thought in Peter of Bergamo's
supplement to the *Summa Theologiae*, deals with the perfections of the
risen body *common* to the blessed and the reprobate before he treats
the differences between their final bodily states. In this sense even the
damned share in a certain *consociatio* insofar as resurrection is an
objective benefit for their human nature. It is as though God gives in
Christ as much as any man will accept. Thus the resurrection of the
damned is a poignant vindication of the ways of his Providence. The
damned receive only what their nature *must* accept, while personally
rejecting the Supreme Good who offers them eternal life. Thus it is
that they do not experience the Resurrection as a *personal* benefit,
unlike the blessed and those in Limbo whose wills embrace or do not
oppose this great boon to fallen nature.

30 C. Journet, *La Volonté divine salvifique*, op. cit., p. 184. Cardinal
Celestine Sfrondrati, cited above, held a similar position in the seventeenth century against the Jansenists and philo-Jansenists. He held
that the universal salvific will of God was vindicated in the case of
persons in Limbo since the Providence of God in their regard *ad*

Christi merita et redemptionem pertinet 'pertains to Christ's merits and redemption': thus his *Nodus praedestinationis dissolutus,* op. cit., p. 364. Bossuet tried to have his book condemned at Rome for this and several other of his opinions. However, the Holy Office had given the work *censura praevia,* as was necessary at the time since it dealt with questions of actual grace.

31 IV Esdras, 2:30–32 (in critical vernacular versions, II Esdras, 2:30–32).

7

Aborted infants as martyrs: are there wider implications?

Brian Harrison, o.s.
Pontifical Catholic University of Puerto Rico

Mindful of the criteria by which the Pope and other successors of the Apostles would have to judge this question, I have decided to explore one of the many questions which would certainly be prominent in their minds: namely, that of whether *this* proposed development of Catholic doctrine would imply other developments as well. For to the extent that arguments for the claiming of aborted babies as martyrs would logically lead to the opening of other doors hitherto considered closed – or at least, not considered open – by the Church's teaching authority and/or Tradition, the Supreme Pastor of the Church and the chief pastors of the local churches can be expected to respond with a proportionate reserve and caution. As the saying goes, an argument that proves too much proves nothing.

This point will be reinforced if we reflect that the solemn proclamation of aborted infants as martyrs would be a special kind of canonization, according to the common teaching of Catholic theologians, and involves the Church's charism of infallibility. The Magisterium, therefore, can be expected to require conclusive, demonstrative arguments in favour of this thesis as a condition of proclaiming its truth by a solemn act: arguments in favour of its *probable* truth will not be sufficient. This would be a further reason why, in a study destined for the attention of the Supreme Pontiff and the other bishops, responsible theologians could scarcely recommend that class A of persons be raised to the altars of the Church, while deliberately concealing their understanding that such a course of action would also imply a similar elevation for classes B and C as well. Assuming such wider implications could be demonstrated, that fact would need to be made explicit in the recommendation, so as to facilitate the Magisterium's judgment as to whether a solemn or infallible proclamation could be made about any or all of these three classes.

A. Two Distinct Questions: Are they *martyrs?* Are they *saints?*

By way of preliminary clarification, it should be stressed that the question of whether the victims of abortion can be considered and declared as *martyrs* should not be confused with the more general question of whether they can be considered and declared as *saved*, i.e., whether or not we can know that they join the saints in the enjoyment of eternal beatitude.

The answer to the second question could in turn depend on how one answers the still wider question regarding the destiny of babies *in general* who die (whether before or after birth) without receiving the waters of baptism. The most recent treatment of this issue by the Church's Magisterium, *The Catechism of the Catholic Church*, leaves the question unresolved. On the one hand no. 1261 and no. 1283 allow us (but do not *require* us) to *hope* that such infants may be saved, while no. 1257 recalls that we do not *know* that they are saved, telling us that 'The Church does not *know* of any means other than Baptism that *assures* entry into eternal beatitude' [emphasis added]. If we knew that in fact nobody who dies in infancy goes to Limbo (much less to Hell), then the question of whether aborted babies are saved would *ipso facto* be answered in the affirmative. But whether or not anyone goes to Limbo,[1] the question of whether aborted infants enter Heaven *precisely as martyrs* will remain as an independent and pertinent question.

The Catechism of the Catholic Church treats of martyrdom under the general heading of the Eighth Commandment, dealing with our duties regarding truth: 'Martyrdom is the supreme witness given to the truth of the faith ... The martyr ... bears witness to the truth of the faith and of Christian doctrine' (no. 2473). The words 'and of Christian doctrine', which encompass, of course, truths of the natural moral law as well as supernaturally revealed truth, indicate the grounds on which such saints as Maria Goretti and John the Baptist have been declared martyrs: they were not killed *in odium Christi,* but as witnesses to moral principles knowable independently of Christian revelation. Here, however, a distinction should be made between naturally knowable truths of the practical and speculative orders respectively. According to the classical canonical treatise of Pope Benedict XIV, which has governed the Church's practice for more than two centuries,[2] the Church does not canonize those who are slain for upholding naturally knowable speculative truths such as the existence of God or the immortality of the soul. However, in the practical order, many acts of virtue required by the natural moral law, such as the observance of chastity, are also prescribed by Christian revelation as such, and so can qualify those who practise them for martyrdom.[3] Hence Maria Goretti was canonized as a martyr, sacrificing her life to preserve her chastity.

On the other hand, not every saint who sacrifices his/her life for a noble cause, or who is killed unjustly, is a martyr. Saint Joan of Arc, popularly considered a martyr, is not in fact recognized as such by the Church. In the liturgical calendar (Feast-day May 30, in France) she appears simply as 'Saint Joan of Arc, Virgin', not 'Virgin and Martyr'. Joan was sent to the stake not *in odium Christi*, but ostensibly for the very opposite reason, *in nomine Christi*! Her alleged crime was heresy – treason against Christ – while, of course, what really fuelled the zeal of her persecutors was political passion in time of war: she was in effect killed *in odium Francorum*.

In the light of our preliminary clarification above, at least one objection to the comparison with the Holy Innocents can be seen to have no weight. Some Catholics have suggested that there is no true parallel between the Holy Innocents and aborted babies, because the former, as circumcised Jewish children under the Old Covenant dispensation, would in any case have been assured of eternal salvation even if their death in infancy had occurred in any other way, or for any other reason. But, as we have stressed, the question before us is not whether any of the infants under discussion – born or pre-born – are (or would have been) saved or not; the question is whether they are saved *as martyrs*. The most that could be said in virtue of the difference between Old and New Covenants is that the Holy Innocents killed by Herod should not be thought of as receiving a Baptism of blood (because Baptism of any sort was not at that time prescribed for anybody), whereas *if* the victims of abortion (at least since Pentecost, when the Law of Christ was promulgated and came into effect) are not only saved, but saved *as martyrs*, then their violent death would have to be seen as a Baptism of blood.

B. Would the thesis *per se* open other doors as well?

If aborted infants are to be judged and officially claimed by the Church as martyrs comparable to the Holy Innocents, it would seem, on the face of it, that the case for thus claiming them would have to be based on their being witnesses in some way to the Fifth Commandment – 'Thou shalt not kill!' – as Maria Goretti died witnessing to the Sixth Commandment. Let us consider first whether the very fact of claiming the aborted infants as martyrs to the Fifth Commandment, irrespective of whatever particular argument(s) might be used to justify that claim, would imply a similar claim for other classes of human beings.

If we say, for instance, that aborted babies are martyrs to the Fifth Commandment, and are thus killed *in odium fidei* (since revelation as well as natural law gives us the Decalogue), would we then have to say that *all* victims of murder are martyrs? If the murderer's contempt for the Fifth Commandment is sufficient to qualify a *pre-born* victim for martyrdom, why does not that same contempt bestow the same status on a *post-born* victim as well? Indeed, the contempt is arguably more obvious when, in the case of post-born victims, nobody can even pretend that said victim is 'not human'.

Part of the answer to this question would be that, at least in the case of adults, the murderer's defiance of the Fifth Commandment is not the only condition necessary for the conferral of martyr status on his victim. To begin with, the Church has always required as a further condition, from those capable of using free will, a *voluntary act* of heroism in opting for death. Let us suppose, then, an adult who heroically defies an aggressor's threats and is thus murdered, voluntarily sacrificing his life. But let us further suppose circumstances wherein this bravery is fuelled by the desire to save the life of his wife or child, or by his unwillingness to betray his country in a just war. The Church will still not consider this kind of death, however noble in itself, as sufficient for recognition as a martyr. For, even supposing such a victim to be Christian and Catholic, his act of love for country or family member does not necessarily manifest *a love of God above all things* at the moment of death. And that, of course, is the kind of love which is necessary in order to be in the state of grace and so be saved. It may well be possible, psychologically, to lay down one's life for family or fatherland while still failing to repent of certain mortal sins. St Paul suggests this in saying, 'If I should deliver my body to be burned, and have not charity, it profiteth me nothing' (I Cor. 13:3). The Church, at least, could never be so sure that supernatural charity was present in such cases as to canonize those concerned as martyrs, solely on the basis of their voluntarily accepted death. In contrast, the classic or archetypal martyr, namely, a person with the use of reason who voluntarily faces death rather than repudiate or disobey *God's revealed truth*, and who is slain precisely for not repudiating or disobeying it, is taken to manifest by that very fact his love for God above all things, including his very life: a heroic act of supernatural charity.

Canonizing aborted children as martyrs to the Fifth Commandment would not, then, commit the Church logically to canonizing as martyrs all Catholics who voluntarily accept death at the hands of murderous aggressors (much less those who are murdered *in*voluntarily).

But let us narrow the field again. Would any argument for recognizing children slain before birth as martyrs also be an argument for granting the same recognition to all victims of infanticide? (I will define this term, for the sake of convenience and brevity, as the direct killing of children *after* their birth, but before they attain the use of reason.[4]) Would there be any relevant distinction between these two classes of victims? No more than the pre-born are post-born infants capable of either voluntary acts of virtue or personal acts of sin. It is true that in many specific cases – for instance, cases of children slain at around 5–9 years of age – only God (as distinct from the Church) would know for sure whether this or that child had *in fact* attained a sufficient use of reason to be capable of a truly free decision for or against God. But this element of human uncertainty would not in itself be pertinent for present purposes. The proposal before us is that the Church recognize globally as martyrs all aborted children *as a class*; and such recognition could in no way logically imply that the Church attempt to discern the eternal destiny of individual children slain after birth. The most that it could possibly imply would be a similar ecclesial recognition for the victims of infanticide *as a class*, leaving to God the discernment of who, in doubtful cases, belonged to that class.

But does it in fact imply even this? I am inclined to think not. In regard to the motivation of the killers – a factor which the Church certainly takes into account in deciding whether their victims are martyrs or not – there would seem to be a relevant difference, at least in some cases, between abortion and infanticide, and this would be sufficient to rule out any 'blanket' assertions of complete moral equivalence between the two classes of crimes and their respective victims.

In the case of unborn children, no killer can ever be motivated by hatred of the *actions* of his or her victim, since the latter is incapable of *acting* in any way at all which might provoke murderous intentions in either the mother or anyone else. When direct abortion occurs, it is the victim's mere *being* – his or her living existence itself under the given circumstances – which is so abhorred, feared, or despised as to motivate the mother and/or the abortionist to carry out their brutal deed. On the other hand, violence against post-born children on the part of disturbed, malevolent or intoxicated adults (or older children) is quite often provoked by an infant's *action*. Little ones have sometimes been murdered, for instance, by persons in a violent rage provoked by nothing more than a fit of prolonged crying and wailing, or a temper tantrum, on the part of the infant. It may indeed be more frequently the case that infanticide, like abortion, is perpetrated not for any such annoying action on the part of the infant, but simply because his or her very existence is deemed inconvenient by the killer. But the fact that at least some cases of infanticide are occasioned or provoked by action on the part of the victim is sufficient to show that, in regard to the question of what motivates the killer, abortion victims *as a class* cannot simply and indiscriminately be morally equated with infanticide victims *as a class.*

It might be objected, however, that this difference (in some cases) is not of such a kind as to be relevant to the question of whether victims of either class could be declared martyrs or not. After all, the fact that the behaviour of post-born infants can at times be extremely trying does not lessen their subjective personal innocence in comparison with that of the unborn: we are, after all, defining infanticide here to include only those cases wherein the child victims have *not* yet attained the use of reason and moral responsibility. While this is certainly true, subjective innocence is not the only relevant factor here. The action of a two-year-old tot throwing a temper tantrum, while not morally blameworthy, can fairly be seen as objectively disordered activity; and the disorder cannot be explained otherwise than as one of the many sad results of original sin. Precisely for that reason, it would be very difficult to see how one who murders a child in that situation could be said to act *in odium Christi,* even implicitly. What arouses his fury (criminally and insanely excessive though it is) is not something good or holy in itself, but behaviour which is symptomatic of our race's tragic fall from original justice.

We may conclude, then, on the basis of these pertinent differences between abortion and infanticide, that a papal canonization or claiming of all victims of abortion as martyrs would not logically require a similar elevation of all victims of infanticide (and much less of all Catholic adults who heroically accept an unjust death) to the altars of the Church as martyrs. Such a papal act would certainly imply that *many* victims of infanticide are in fact martyrs; but in view of the relative complexities, and perhaps uncertainties, involved in deciding and defining *which* infanticide victims would qualify for that privilege, the Church's supreme authority would not be at all inconsistent, and indeed, would be entirely reasonable and prudent, in choosing to remain silent, at least for the time being, on that point.

C. Would some specific arguments for the thesis open other doors?

Supposing we are correct in maintaining that the claiming of aborted children as martyrs would not, *in itself*, logically commit the Church to a canonization of other entire classes of slain persons as well, it remains to be considered whether any of the *specific arguments* advanced for their martyr status would have more radical implications of that sort.

One argument for considering the victims of abortions as martyrs is to see them as icons of the divine innocence of the Christ Child, who is hated as such by Satan, the ultimate instigator of those who slay the unborn. In that way they are seen more clearly as being killed *in odium Christi*, like the original Holy Innocents. In an article on this question, for instance, John F. McCarthy asks, 'Would God ever give to Satan the power by acts of murder to rob unborn children of any chance to receive the saving grace of Christ?'[5] That is certainly a provocative and pertinent question; but if we give the rhetorically expected negative answer to it, it is by no means easy to see why a similar answer would not be required to such further questions as to whether God would allow persons *other* than Satan, or even circumstances not positively willed by anyone, to 'rob' infants, whether born or unborn – and whether by acts of murder or by simple failure to baptize them – 'of any chance to receive the saving grace of Christ'. At bottom, the question, at least in the form posed by McCarthy, seems to be whether God's Providence would permit the loss of eternal salvation for *anyone* who dies without ever having reached the capacity to choose personally for or against God. So what is presented in the first instance as an argument for the martyr status of aborted babies is implicitly an argument for the salvation of unbaptized infants *in general* (i.e., for abandoning belief in Limbo). And that would need to made clear in any recommendation destined for evaluation and judgement by the Pope and bishops.

There are, moreover, other reasons why *Satan's* hatred of unborn infants would seem to be a weak reed to lean upon if we are looking for conclusive evidence for their status as martyrs. The argument is that the evil spirit has a particular abhorrence for these infants as 'icons' of the Christ child. But, in the first place, second-guessing the Devil as to which persons he hates more than others would, I think, be a risky venture. I doubt that we can reason theoretically and deductively about the will of Satan with the same kind of confidence that theologians show in reasoning about the will of God, which is perfectly good and perfectly consistent. Evidence garnered empirically and inductively from the experience of exorcists suggests that Satan and the other fallen Angels are now to some extent capricious and unpredictable.

Secondly, the Church has always taken it for granted that in the case of martyrs slain *in odium Christi*, or *in odium fidei*, the *odium* in question has to be that of the person or persons who actually slays the victim, functioning as an efficient or at least moral cause of his or her death. But it is not in fact Satan who either kills, or orders the killing of, the victims of abortion. His role as tempter and inspirer of evil designs does not allow us to attribute to him that function. The popular slogan of some years ago, 'The Devil made me do it!' is theologically incorrect to the extent that it is understood as attributing irresistible power over man's free will to the Evil One. Nor does the aborting mother or doctor stand in as close a relation to Satan as the executioners at Bethlehem stood in relation to Herod. That is, they are not (except perhaps in unusual cases of occult-related abortions) mere agents or hired instruments of Satan carrying out his orders. Only in the case of a murder committed by a person thoroughly possessed – that is, a person whose *body* (not soul) is temporarily dominated and moved by Satan – could we speak of the latter as being the author of the crime in the sense that is pertinent here.

Finally, it is far from clear to me that the potential victims of abortion, who are still in original sin, deprived of grace, and to that extent under Satan's own dominion, are, simply by virtue of not yet having committed any personal sin, better 'icons' of Christ than baptized persons who have the use of reason and are in the state of grace. After all, it is precisely Baptism which conforms us to, incorporates us into, and makes us images (icons) of, Christ Himself. Therefore, even supposing for the sake of argument that the will of Satan were entirely predictable and consistent, it seems highly debatable whether unborn infants would be an object of greater abhorrence to him than many good Christians with the use of reason, especially those who have already attained a high level of sanctity. Hence, if aborted children are to be declared to have died *in odium Christi* (and thus, canonized as martyrs) because Satan – presumably – sees and hates Christ in them, it is not easy to see how we could avoid claiming martyr status, on the same or even stronger grounds, for any holy Christian who heroically accepts an unjust death. St Joan of Arc would be a case in point. But, as we have already noted, the Church decided against canonizing Saint Joan *as a martyr.*

In short, introducing Satan into the argument for the martyr status of aborted children seems problematical for various reasons – one of the problems being that this would seem to be another case of opening a door which logically opens other hitherto closed doors. If aborted children are to be claimed as martyrs, it will have to be because the *human beings* responsible for their slaughter render them witnesses to Christ in some way.

What other avenues can be explored? Approved Catholic theology – although never so far officially ratified by the Magisterium – has long held that an unborn infant who dies when its mother is killed for the faith receives the Baptism of blood, and can be considered a martyr along with the mother herself. As regards infants, says the author of the article 'Martyre' in the *Dictionnaire de Théologie catholique*, '... *il suffit qu'ils soient morts pour le Christ et cela même dans le sein maternel*' ('it is enough that they have died for Christ and that even in their mother's womb').[6] In such cases the *odium* of the killers is directed explicitly only at the Christian faith or behaviour of the mother, and so only in an indirect or implicit way can the unborn infant – of whose very existence the mother's executioner may well be unaware – be said to die 'for Christ'.

But, if that indirect or implicit link to Christ is sufficient to claim these unborn victims of *overtly* anti-Christian persecution as martyrs along with the Holy Innocents, could not another kind of indirect link be discerned, and considered sufficient, in the case of aborted children? For they too are the victims of an anti-Christian mentality: disregard of, and even contempt for, the Fifth Commandment. It is true that those who destroy unborn infants are not always overtly or explicitly anti-Christian in the way persecutors of the faith are: some, indeed, are churchgoers who try to harmonize or rationalize their faith and their consciences with the practice of abortion. But this consideration would seem to be balanced in the scales by the fact that the victim status, as such, of aborted children is *more* overt and explicit than that of the unborn children of martyred women. In abortion the infant's death is (by definition) directly and principally willed, whereas in the case of persecution the unborn infant's death would usually be willed, if at all, only indirectly – that is, as a foreseeable consequence or side-effect of slaying the mother.

I have already referred to the fact that, in abortion, as distinct from the murder of adults, or even infanticide, it can never be any *action* on the part of the potential victim, only the mere fact of his *existence* – his very life – that provokes the violence of his assailant. Here I believe we can discern a genuine basis for seeing all abortions as acts implicitly directed against Christ. The living unborn child, even though not yet definitively and supernaturally incorporated into Christ by the grace of Baptism, is not only ordered to that incorporation by virtue of the universal salvific will of God, but is already, at the natural level, created in the image of God, and thus, by virtue of the incarnation, in the image of God the Son, who took flesh in Mary's womb and made himself in a certain way the 'brother' of every unborn child. Now, in every case of direct abortion, at least one (and at times all) of those responsible – the mother, the abortionist, or perhaps other instigators or accomplices – rejects or despises to the point of wilful destruction this human life *as such*. That is, we have in every such case the decision of a killer which is motivated not by any real or imagined *offence* that could constitute the formal object of his or her contempt and rejection, and which would (if real) besmirch or obscure the divine image to some extent, but *by nothing more than the fact that victim is a living individual – consciously recognized as actually or at least potentially a human person – who happens to exist when and where no human person at all is wanted.* Thus, the act of abortion not only betrays rejection or scorn for the divine *law* which forbids killing of the innocent; it also involves an objective (though perhaps unconscious) rejection or scorn for the divine *Person* in whose image the innocent victim is made, precisely insofar as the assailant himself or herself *does not and cannot deny* the total innocence of the victim. In short, in despising an avowedly innocent life, the one who aborts implicitly despises Innocence itself, the divine Innocence, and Life itself – Christ our Life.

Among the Scriptural references found in the recent writings on this subject which have been presented by Mrs Patricia de Menezes, one which occurs repeatedly, and which would seem to have the clearest and most pertinent application to the present question, is a citation from the parable of the Last Judgement: 'Inasmuch as you did it to one of these, the least of my brethren, you did it to me'. *Quamdiu fecistis uni de his fratribus meis minimis, mihi fecistis* (Matt. 25:

40). Even though these words refer in their original context explicitly only to those who do good, not evil, to the poor and suffering, the same parable's expressed judgement against those who merely *neglect* the plight of such needy persons (vv. 41–45) implies that, with still greater reason, those who do not just neglect, but positively *attack and oppress*, the poor and needy will find on the Day of Judgement that they were thereby attacking and oppressing Christ himself. It is therefore, exegetically speaking, perfectly reasonable to apply the words of v. 40 to evil as well as charitable actions. Also, there is no indication in the text that either circumcision or baptism is laid down as a prerequisite for being considered by Our Lord as one of his 'brethren' in the sense which is relevant here. That is, one does not have to be fully incorporated into the People of God to enjoy unwittingly this kind of solidarity with the Son of Man; it is enough to be hungry, thirsty, naked, exiled, sick, or imprisoned (cf. vv. 35–38, 42–44). Hence, taking into account the personhood of the unborn, it would seem impossible, in any serious, rational, and authentically Catholic reading of the Gospel, to exclude the victims of abortion from the class of poor and downtrodden with whom Jesus identifies himself here. No brethren are 'littler', more naked, more defenceless, or more totally needy, than these! Even their home, the womb, is turned into a 'prison' of the worst kind – a death chamber – by the abortionist!

Indeed, the Church's Magisterium now guarantees the authenticity of such an exegesis of the Gospel passage under discussion. The 1995 Encyclical *Evangelium Vitae* expressly includes 'the unborn child'[7] among the vulnerable, poor and marginalized with whom Our Lord identifies himself in Matthew 25:40, and, citing that very text in the title of the entire concluding section of this document on the sacredness of human life,[8] John Paul II goes on to apply it precisely to the killing of the innocent. After observing (in article 104) that the newborn child of Apocalypse 12:4, object of the dragon's murderous hatred, is in certain way a figure of every child, not only of the Christ-child, the Pope affirms the following as an implication of the Incarnation:

Precisely in the 'flesh' of every man, Christ continues to reveal himself and to enter into communion with us, so that *the rejection of human life*, in its various forms, is *really the rejection of Christ*. This is the fascinating, and at the same time demanding, truth which Christ makes known to us and which his Church tirelessly continues to teach: 'He who receives a child like this in my name, receives me' (Mt. 18: 5); 'In truth I tell you, that when you did it to one of these, the least of my brethren, you did it to me' (Mt. 25:40).[9]

I would venture to conclude, then, that it is *theologically certain,* because ascertainable by the application of reason to truths revealed in Scripture, that even though aborted children are not necessarily slain consciously and explicitly *in odium Christi*, as were the Holy Innocents of Bethlehem, they are slain *in odium Christi* from the *implicit* viewpoint of their killers, who, by slaying them, manifest their wilful and total rejection of an innocent human life as such, and hence for its Author – who is also the Author of the Fifth Commandment. Perhaps most importantly of all, **their *odium* has Christ as its object from the conscious and explicit viewpoint of Christ himself**, as will be manifested at the Last Judgement. Therefore, it will be a legitimate development of doctrine for the Magisterium to recognize their Baptism of blood and their status as martyrs by a formal act. Such a development would not appear to be a greater 'innovation' than that previous development by which the Holy Innocents themselves were recognized as martyrs, several centuries after public revelation ceased. Like that development, the claiming of aborted children as martyrs may imply a certain broadening of the concept of martyrdom, but precedents for this already exist: as well as the recognition of the Holy Innocents themselves, the canonization of St Maximilian Kolbe as a martyr entailed a certain novelty, insofar as he was killed by the Nazis as a voluntary substitute for another prisoner who was to have been executed for reasons quite independent of any explicit *odium fidei*. And the Church at least since the medieval era has recognized the Blessed Virgin as a martyr of an extraordinary kind – indeed, as 'Queen of Martyrs' – by virtue of the mystical 'sword' which was to pierce her soul (Luke 2:35) even though she did not die a violent death of any sort.[10]

It needs to be asked, however, in accordance with the general methodology pursued in this essay, whether the argument from Matthew 25 will, assuming it is valid, imply martyr status for other groups as well as aborted children. Would the argument also imply similar recognition as martyrs for all Christians in the state of grace who voluntarily accept an unjustly inflicted death, even when such oppression is motivated by some 'secular' passion rather than enmity against the true religion? One thinks again of the execution of Saint Joan of Arc as a kind of test case. Certainly, on the basis of Matthew 25, we will have to acknowledge that Our Lord is surely in firm solidarity with such persons in their hour of innocent suffering and will accept what is done to them as *in some sense* done to himself. Moreover, since, *ex hypothesi*, they are in the state of grace at the time of death, they will certainly be saved. But the question is whether in Heaven such holy and heroic victims of 'secular' injustice will have the *aureola* of martyrdom or not. The Church has traditionally – though not infallibly – answered that question in the negative, as we noted at the outset.

It seems to me that the parallel between this class of victims and the class of aborted infants is not so close that the argument from Matthew 25 will necessarily apply to the former as much as the latter. It seems that the *odium* of those who kill the unborn is seen more clearly as *odium Christi*, in the context of this Gospel parable as in the more general context we considered earlier, precisely because the perpetrators of abortion themselves cannot even pretend that the one they destroy is in any degree 'guilty' of any offence that might even in some minimal way 'deserve' death. They are knowingly assailing life itself, something good in itself. However, in many or most cases of unjust 'secular' homicide, the killer bears a hatred directed consciously to some real or imagined offence on the part of the victim: and to the extent that these vengeful, avaricious, or politically partisan hatreds are explicitly directed toward something or someone other than Jesus Christ and his Gospel, that fact may well, for all we know, affect the precise extent or manner in which Our Lord identifies himself with the victim.

For the reasons already outlined, similar considerations will perhaps apply (though only minimally, if at all) to the victims of infanticide – whether or not such children were sacramentally baptized before death. The argument we have used from Matthew 25 will certainly and obviously mean that *most* infants slain after birth, but before attaining the use of reason, are martyrs in Heaven along with the victims of abortion. It may well be that *all* of them attain the martyrs' crown, but since there could be an element of uncertainty in some cases, the Church's teaching authority would be justified, at least in the present state of theological reflection and doctrinal development, in limiting its formal proclamation to the martyr status of aborted babies.

I hope to have shown in these pages that a sound argument can be made for the claiming of aborted children[11] as martyr companions of the Holy Innocents: an argument which would **not** logically commit the Church to making a similar claim for other whole groups of slain persons, and much less to abandoning belief in Limbo as such.

Appendix: Magisterial statements on the eternal destiny of Aborted Infants

After having completed the above essay arguing for the martyr status of aborted infants, this writer became aware of two pertinent interventions of the Church's Magisterium which will need to be taken into account in evaluating that conclusion.

Many Catholics familiar with Pope John Paul II's 1995 Encyclical *Evangelium Vitae* are still unaware of the fact that in the definitive version of this document, published in *Acta Apostolicae Sedis*, the Pontiff withdrew a statement found in the initially published version of article 99 to the effect that women who have had abortions can 'ask pardon' of the child in question, 'who now lives in the Lord'. That sentence has now been replaced by the following advice to such mothers: 'You can entrust your infant with hope to the same Father and to his mercy.'[12] This aligns the position of the Encyclical with that of *The Catechism of the Catholic Church* (nos. 1257, 1261 and 1283), and the Church's funeral Liturgy for unbaptized infants: a position of reserve and uncertainty regarding the destiny of such infants.

As a result of this revision of the recent Encyclical, there is now no statement of the Church's Magisterium which either states or implies that aborted infants definitely attain eternal salvation. Prompted by his discovery of this change in the text of *Evangelium Vitae*, this writer made further efforts to research what other successors of Peter may have said on the subject. It appears that the only other papal statement dealing expressly with the destiny of aborted infants is that of Pope Sixtus V, whose Constitution *Effraenatam* of 29 October 1588 not only abstains from raising any hopes that they may attain the beatific vision, but positively affirms that they do *not* attain it.

The main purpose of this document is to reinforce civil and canonical sanctions against those who carry out abortions and sterilizations: it goes so far as to prescribe the death penalty for these offences. The Pope begins by affirming the need for sterner measures to be taken against 'the barbarity ... of those who do not shrink from the most cruel slaughter of fetuses still coming to maturity in the shelter of their mothers' wombs.'[13] He then continues, by way of explanation:

For who would not detest a crime as execrable as this – a crime whose consequence is that not just bodies, but – still worse! – even souls, are, as it were, cast away? The soul of the unborn infant bears the imprint of God's image! It is a soul for whose redemption Christ our Lord shed His precious blood, a soul capable of eternal blessedness and destined for the company of Angels! Who, therefore, would not condemn and punish with the utmost severity the desecration committed by one who has excluded such a soul from the blessed vision of God? Such a one has done all he or she could possibly have done to prevent this soul from reaching the place prepared for it in heaven, and has deprived God of the service of this His own creature.[14]

These expressions certainly do not constitute an *ex cathedra* definition, and indeed, the Constitution itself is primarily a legislative act – an exercise of the Pope's governing authority rather than his teaching authority. Nevertheless, in view of the clarity and force of the Pontiff's teaching, in this preamble to the legislative norms which form the main body of the document, it is arguable that the doctrinal proposition in question – namely, that the souls of aborted infants are excluded·from the beatific vision – should be seen as belonging (at least at that time) to the authentic, although non-infallible, teaching of Peter's successor.

Another possible interpretation of *Effraenatam*, however, would also seem arguable. It is noteworthy that Sixtus V does not present the proposition under discussion as one which is being currently disputed, and which needs reaffirmation for that very reason; rather, it is enunciated as a truth which he expects will be *taken for granted* by all faithful Catholics, and which he wishes to reiterate here chiefly in order to remind them of an additional reason as to why the severest possible penalties should be applied to those guilty of killing the unborn. But the legislative rather than magisterial purpose of the document as a whole, together with the apparent absence of controversy at that time in regard to the destiny of aborted children, could perhaps entitle us to view the Pope's statement that they are excluded from the beatific vision not as an expression of authentic Catholic doctrine, but simply as a repetition of the commonly accepted theological opinion of that time. It is relevant that this papal statement appears to be a completely isolated one. If indeed it were the irreformable (or even merely authentic) doctrine of the Church that aborted infants are excluded from the vision of God, it would seem strange, given the Church's clear and perennial understanding that the loss of Heaven is a far greater deprivation than the loss of temporal life, that this doctrine has not been repeated with far greater frequency and urgency than in fact it has been, in the context of magisterial statements against abortion.

There have been many such statements on the part of the Fathers, Councils and Popes,[15] but on no occasion other than in this 1588 Constitution, it seems, has the Magisterium enunciated this pessimistic prognosis regarding the destiny of aborted infants. Pope Pius XI, for example, in condemning abortion extensively in his 1930 Encyclical *Casti Connubii*, bases his argumentation exclusively on the Fifth Commandment and the infant's consequent right to *temporal* life.[16] That is, he is totally silent in regard to the infant's eternal destiny, even though this encyclical was published at a time when few if any Catholic theologians were questioning the view that (at least as a general rule) infants who die without sacramental Baptism are denied the beatific vision. It is almost as if some inchoate hesitation or perplexity, fuelled by a certain unformulated sense of compassion for these tiny victims (perhaps it is that 'logic of love' which some theologians appeal to?) has led the great majority of the Church's pastors over the centuries to shrink from applying that 'general rule' openly, explicitly and remorselessly to the case of infants slain before birth, and to prefer instead complete reticence regarding their eternal destiny.

Notes

[1] This writer's present opinion, based on the weight of constant Church tradition and on his reading of weighty magisterial statements such as those of the Council of Florence, is that at least some persons do in fact die in original sin, but without personal mortal sin, and so neither suffer the pains of hell nor enjoy the beatific vision. If there are, among such persons, some whose lack of baptism was not due, even remotely, to any sinful act or omission on the part of others, their eternal condition could still be reconciled with 'the universal salvific will of God' if we understand that doctrine to mean, not that God wills the beatific vision for all men without exception, but that he wills that all without exception at least be saved from the fires of hell and attain eternal happiness (natural or supernatural as the case may be).

[2] *De servorum Dei beatificatione et beatorum canonizatione* (Bologna 1737).

[3] DTC, Vol. X. I, col. 232.

[4] Such a definition has the disadvantage, of course, of not including the victims of abortion, and thus, perhaps, seeming to imply that these are not truly 'infants'. But it is useful to have a single word with which to distinguish between pre-born and post-born victims of murderous acts, and 'infanticide' seems to be the only one available to describe the latter.

5 J. F. McCarthy, 'Further Reflections on the Claiming of Aborted Children', *Living Tradition* 71 (July–September 1977), p. 2.

6 DTC, Vol X, col. 227.

7 '… *etiam infantem nondum natum*' John Paul II, Encyclical *Evangelium Vitae*, 87 (*AAS* 87 [1995] p. 500).

8 Cf. Chapter 4, entitled '"You did it to me": towards a new culture of human life', ibid., p. 490.

9 '*In "carne" scilicet cuique hominis Christus pergit se ostendere et nobiscum communionem coniungere, ideoque <u>hominis vitæ repudiatio</u> variis suis sub formis <u>reapse ipsius Christi est repudiatio</u>. Hæc tandem mirifica est ac imperiosa simul veritas quam nobis Christus aperit et eius Ecclesia iterum iterumque indefessa repetit: "Quis susceperit unum parvulum talem in nomine meo, me suscipit" (Mt. 18, 5); "Amen dico vobis, quamdiu fecistis uni de minimis meis, mihi fecistis"* (Mt. 25, 40)' (ibid., p. 521, emphasis in original).

10 In the Liturgy of the Hours for the Feast of Our Lady of Sorrows (September 15) the entire second reading for the Office of Readings consists of St Bernard's exposition of Mary's martyrdom, while at Vespers that day the Church sings in the Responsory, '*Felix est illa, quæ sine morte meruit palmam martyrii*': 'Blessed is she who without dying earned the palm of martyrdom'.

11 The wording of any such official declaration could not ignore the Church's lack of certainty as to whether the fetus has a soul – and is thus a human person – right from the moment of fertilization. The term 'victims of abortion' would not be suitable (for a sub-human creature can also be a 'victim'). The wording would need to specify as martyrs those 'infants,' 'children,' or 'persons' slain by abortion.

12 '*Infantem autem vestrum potestis Eidem Patri Eiusque misericordiae cum spe committere*' (*AAS* 87 [1995], p. 515).

13 '… *eorum immanitatem … qui immaturos foetus intra materna viscera adhuc latentes crudelissime necare non verentur*' (P. Gasparri [ed.], *Codex Iuris Canonici, Fontes*, vol. I (Rome: Vatican Polyglot Press, 1923), p. 308).

14 '*Quis enim non detestetur, tam execrandum facinus, per quod nedum corporum, sed quod gravius est, etiam animarum certa iactura sequitur? Quis non gravissimis suppliciis damnet illius impietatem, qui animam Dei imagine insignitam, pro qua redimenda Christus Dominus noster preciosum Sanguinem fudit, aeternae capacem Beatitudinis, et ad consortium Angelorum destinatam, a beata Dei visione exclusit, reparationem coelestium sedium quantum in ipso fuit, impedivit, Deo servitium suae creaturae ademit?*' (ibid).

15 Cf. for example the review of such monuments of Tradition in A. Fernández, *Teologia Moral*, vol. II (Burgos: Ediciones Aldecoa, 1993), pp 684–693.

16 Cf. DH 3719–3721.

8

Holy Innocents in our times

Philippe Jobert, O.S.B.
Abbey of St. Pierre de Solesmes, France

Can the Magisterium of the Church recognize little children slain by abortion as companions of the Holy Innocents and therefore as martyrs?

If the reply to this question is affirmative, it follows that these child victims of procured abortion are sharers in the divine glory in Heaven. We must, then, by way of preliminary, resolve another problem. How could these children, who by definition have been unable to receive Baptism, enter into the glory of which the grace received at Baptism is the necessary condition?

A. Glory

Arguments may be put forward to prove that glory is fitting to these children:

Firstly, they are images of God, having a spiritual soul from the first moment of their conception.

Secondly, they are innocent, having committed no actual sin. Only original sin deprives them of supernatural justice, such that their natural will is not ordered to the beatific vision.

Thirdly, by violence they have been deprived of human birth and in that way of Baptism which is the ordinary means of salvation.

Fourthly, in glory they are innumerable living voices praising the gratuitous mercy of God; they are intercessors for their murderers and for all sinners.

The glory that it is fitting to ascribe to infants slain by abortion is also fitting to God. For, firstly, Holy Scripture reveals his universal saving plan (Matt. 18:14; I. Tim. 2:4; II Pet. 3:9), to which the souls of aborted children oppose no obstacle. Secondly, the cases of Jeremiah (Jer. 1:5) and St John the Baptist (Luke 1:15) show that God is free graciously to sanctify an infant in his mother's womb.

The like case of Mary is a dogma of faith: the Immaculate Conception. Thirdly, Christ poured out his blood and gave his life on the Cross for all men. Being the Creator, he precontains all creatures pre-existently within himself. With him who is a divine Person subsisting in an individual human nature, all the human beings who pre-exist in this divine Person subsist in this individual human nature. Thus when Christ acts, suffers and dies, all men act, suffer and die in him and with him. Among this host, aborted children are saved virtually. To be saved actually all that is needful is for the grace of God to be accorded them before their own deaths, since they have already died virtually in Christ on the Cross. Fourthly, Christ affirmed on several occasions that little ones and children are dearest to his heart. Since his power as Saviour is not limited to the sacraments, he anticipates for these preferred recipients the gift of grace they are unable to receive in another manner.

And yet the most powerful argument from fittingness which can be invoked in favour of the glory of aborted children seems to be that drawn from the logic of divine Love. Notwithstanding the supreme liberty of God and the gratuitous character of salvation, there is an extremely deep connexion between the mystery of divine Love and the glory of these murdered children. It operates on three levels which correspond to the levels of that Love itself as these can be distinguished by their effects.

First, his Charity-love, by which God loves men as himself, and wants all men to become members of Christ, united to him, conformed by adoptive filiation to Christ's image as the Son of God in glory. Secondly, his Justice-love, by which God wills glory for all men as owing in justice to the Blood Christ poured out for them. Justice-love too for the children, who are cruelly deprived of the ordinary means of salvation. Thirdly, his Mercy-love, by which God gave his only Son as a ransom to death and sin so that all men might be liberated from their wretchedness. And what wretchedness is greater than that of these children? Even the greatest sinners, and among them the abortionists, can at any moment, right up to the last second before their death be converted from their sins by the grace that changes their free will. But these innocent ones, who do not have the use of free will, are bereft even of this possibility.

The God who is Love has created humanity with the gift of natural life, so that it may be the subject of his gratuitous gift of supernatural life. There is in human nature no exigence for the grace which is the life everlasting, nor even a disposition to receive it. There is only the spiritual capacity freely to be raised up to share in the life of the Holy Trinity who infinitely surpass that human nature.

If human life is supernaturally ordered to eternal life, that derives uniquely from the free design of divine Charity drawing human life to itself. If the powers of evil try to interpose obstacles to the plan of God by slaying infants before their birth, those same forces are outclassed by the logic of Love which anticipates the gift of grace before the deaths of their victims. We must not be fearful of exaggeration when we spoke of the Love of God which surpasses all knowledge (Eph. 3:19) and of the power of his desire for the salvation of all, especially favouring the countless innocents killed by abortion.

B. Martyrdom

They are slain, so is it possible to call them martyrs? Martyrdom signifies a testimony given to Jesus Christ, God and man, at the price of human life (*Veritatis Splendor*, no. 93). It is the most heroic act of faith, hope and charity, implying the voluntary preference for eternal life, and the renunciation of earthly life. The martyrs perfectly resemble Christ the King of martyrs who was condemned to death and crucified for his testimony to the truth of his divinity. This likeness to Christ is the ground of an extension of the title of martyr to those who were slain for their relation to Christ, even if they lacked the freedom to choose him. The Holy Innocents were massacred by Herod who wanted to kill Christ: formally speaking, Christ was martyred in each of them. By their blood they were Christ's witnesses as the Messiah, without any possibility of willing this.

We want now to compare to the Holy Innocents the case of children who are victims of abortion. Is there a relation between their deaths and the death of Christ?

Their murderers seek to suppress their filiation visa-à-vis a father and mother. That filiation is an image of the divine filiation of Christ. Furthermore, it is like to the human filiation of him who called himself the Son of Man. However, the murder of aborted children does not have as its aim the suppression of their filiation as such, and so the victims of procured abortion cannot be considered [by this title, q.v.] as martyrs.

The same reply can be made to an argument based on life. Christ said, 'I am the Life' (John 14:6). The life of aborted children is an image of and a participation, however distant, in Christ as Life. But this relation is alien to the intention of abortionists.

We cannot therefore make use of these innocent persons' subjective likeness to Christ as proof of martyrdom.

To be objective, this proof must be sought elsewhere. St Augustine wrote, 'If Christ is the Truth, whosoever is condemned for the truth, suffers for Christ and is crowned with good right'. These words concern St John the Baptist, who was decapitated for the divine truth about marriage. More recently, St Maria Goretti and other virgins have been canonized as martyrs for chastity.

Children killed by abortion are martyrs for the divine truth about life. 'Thou shalt not kill'. This divine command is revealed in Sacred Scripture (Exod. 20:13). It is also inscribed in the heart of every human person, belonging as it does to the natural law. Those who bring to an end the lives of children before their births voluntarily transgress this divine law, and so aborted children are made into victims, in all objectivity, for that law, even though they had no possibility of choosing to die for the truth about life. This objectivity confers on their death the formal status of martyrdom.

Some people may express astonishment that God could accord so high a significance to something as tenuous, fragile and insignificant in the eyes of many as a human embryo at the moment of its conception. However, it has to be borne in mind that Christ poured out his Blood for the soul which gives the embryo its spiritual and bodily life.

Moreover, to grasp the seriousness of the precept, 'Thou shalt not kill', it must not be overlooked that human life is the necessary subject for the reception of the free gift of eternal life. To suppress human life amounts to preventing God from giving grace. In the light of the logic of Love there is no worse crime than to render impossible this connexion between earthly life and life everlasting, a connexion gratuitously established by the free will of God.

By virtue of his universal will to save God provides for the rupture of this connexion by a prior gift of sanctifying grace at the very moment of the murder of aborted infants. These children do indeed belong to the divine Love that saved them on the Cross, when they pre-existed subsistently in his crucified humanity. As embryos, they belong to Christ in a special way, since, lacking the use of their free will, they cannot possess themselves. They have only their human nature, and God rules all created nature in immediate fashion by his Providence. Moreover, they are the closest image of Christ, who was reduced to nothing when he entered this world as an embryo. The Mother of Christ loves these children to whom birth has been denied because, when she gave birth to her divine Son, she gave them also birth at the same time as pre-existing subsistently in him. When they die, Christ, acting in conformity to his divine logic of Love, takes them as members of his Mystical Body, for he lives in them by the grace that flows from his heart. His divine Innocence is crucified when they are slain.

It is Christ himself who, by their death, attests his divine truth about life because their deaths prolong his own death on the Cross. Mary, the mother of the mystical and hidden wounds, becomes then their very own mother. Because Christ is a martyr in them, assuming their deaths as his own, they are really martyrs in Christ. The Church, the Mystical Body of Christ, grants a voice to their testimony and engenders them in proclaiming them martyrs and her children.

In this way, the victory of Christ over sin and death is complete, and is fully manifested by this host beyond all counting of his martyrs. At the same time the greatness of the plan of salvation, the power of the Blood of Christ and the infinitude of the divine mercy which conceived the redemptive scheme, are all proclaimed.

God, then, who created the universe and humankind within it for the glory of his mercy, reveals that mercy in its supreme degree, not only when he grants grace to aborted children before they are deprived of life but also and above all when he gives them the glory of martyrdom since their death is configured to the death of Christ as witness to divine truth. Christ indeed gives testimony in them and dies in them because they cannot use their own free will to offer up their lives.

By their martyrs' deaths they become members of the Mystical Body of the Christ who hallows them. They are sanctified not outwith but within the Church. She is their mother, not by the sacrament of Baptism, but by proclaiming that they are her glorious children through the Baptism of blood. She gives to their blood a voice to proclaim the truth of God about life, the glory of the mercy of God and the power of the Blood of Christ.

Christ himself, as the divine Word living in these glorified children, speaks by their blood as witness to divine truth about life. But Christ as the Word of God lives in the Church when the Church speaks. He proclaims the slain children as members of the Church when she recognizes them as martyrs, identifying their witness with the witness of Christ.

God the Father engenders his Son, expressing himself in his Word. The world has been created by the Word of God (John 1:3) who was made man by Mary's word, *Fiat*. The Word of God gives birth in the Church to murdered infants when this virgin mother proclaims them her glorious children: it is a generation by means of the word. Just so Baptism is a sacred word conjoined with water (Eph. 5:26) which gives birth to the adoptive sons of God. Just as at a christening the parents confess their faith and renounce the works of Satan in the name of their children, so Mother Church, by proclaiming as martyrs children killed through abortion, confesses her faith in the divine truth about life and condemns abortion as a crime.

Thus the direct justification of these children in their mother's womb in no way deprives the Church of her mission of salvation, because this proclamation is a necessary act of the Church if their testimony is going to be heard by everyone. Though they live already in the Lord, they are not yet born into glory so long as the Church has not affirmed that glory. It is by this affirmation which gives them birth in glory that she becomes their mother.

This proclamation is not only a glory for the children but above all for God, for Christ crucified, and for the Church. Their witness glorifies the absolute gratuity of their salvation because they are incapable of freely co-operating therein.

It is also a glory for us since in the Eucharist we are in communion with all those who are 'contained' in Christ, and consequently with these glorious martyrs, the abortion-slain.

9

The Way of the Lamb

John Saward
Plater College, Oxford

Charles Péguy, like St Thérèse of Lisieux and G. K. Chesterton, was given a prophetic insight into the drama of the twentieth century, the 'century of wolves'. In particular, Péguy, like his two companions, was taught by God that the Holy Innocents of Bethlehem had a special significance for the coming darkness.

> Innocents for Christ
> the children were massacred
> (*infantes*, very young children, a tiny child not yet speaking).[1]

God the Father sees all children in his Son, his Son in all children, but the Innocents of Bethlehem resemble the Only-Begotten in a unique way, for they are his contemporaries and compatriots, as well as his comrades in the infant state of his human nature:

> I love them innocently, says God ...
> (That's the way you should love these innocents)
> As a father of a family loves the playmates of his son
> Who go to school with him.[2]

The Holy Innocents of Bethlehem are united with the Son, and confess his Incarnation, simply by the fact of their infancy and the time and place of their birth, and through this bond they are sanctified by the Holy Spirit, dying a death that is true martyrdom, a Baptism in blood that confers the salvific effects of Baptism in water. This is the doctrine of Pope St Leo the Great, preaching on the Solemnity of the Epiphany:

> They were able to die for him whom they could not yet confess. Thus Christ, so that no period of his life should be without miracle, silently exercised the power of the Word

before the use of speech, as if already saying, 'Suffer the little children and forbid them not to come to me, and do not hinder them, for the Kingdom of Heaven is for such' (Matt. 19:14). He crowned infants with a new glory, and consecrated the first days of these little ones by his own beginnings, in order to teach us that no member of the human race is incapable of the divine mystery, since even this age was capable of the glory of martyrdom.[3]

Quoting Prudentius's hymn sung by the Church on their feast day, Péguy shows how the Holy Innocents reveal the true character of Paradise. It is a playground. The Holy Innocents romp in the nurseries of Heaven, in the nursery of God's sons, which is what Heaven is:

Vox prima Christi victima,
Grex immolatorum tener,
Aram sub ipsam simplices
Palma et coronis luditis.
First victim of Christ,
Tender flock of the immolated
Simple at the altar's foot,
Simplices, simple souls, simple children,
Palma et coronis luditis. You play with the palm and the crowns,
With your palm and your crowns.

Such is my paradise, says God. My Paradise is all that is
    simplest.
Nothing is as unpretentious as my paradise
Aram sub ipsam, at the foot of the very altar
These simple children *play* with their palm and their martyrs'
    crowns
That's what goes on in my Paradise.[4]

For Prudentius and Péguy, as also for Dante, the merriment of 'unpretentious' Paradise, the blissful act of beholding the Trinity, is a kind of play.[5] Spiritual childhood is not only the way to Heaven, it is Heaven's very life.

The battle which Péguy fought for innocence and the Innocents still rages. It is the central struggle of our century, compared with which the clash of nations and ideologies are trifling skirmishes. Péguy's call to arms, issued in the spirit of Christian chivalry, defines both the end and the means of the fight. The end is the glory of the Triune God and the defence of the least of Christ's brethren, and the means are the virtues of the Little Way, a child-like exercise of faith, hope, and charity (accompanied, as we have seen, by a manly exercise of the moral virtues). To defend the Innocents we must strive, by God's grace, to be like them. By artless fidelity to the truth in a world of adult deceit, by a humble confidence that disarms the giants of despair, by a prodigal love of the smallest of our brethren, we follow the Lamb wherever he goes. Our simplicity will be our strength.[6] This is the true 'mystery of the charity of Joan of Arc', France's boldest warrior and youngest saint, and it is the final paradox of Péguy's Christian theology of childhood: only the Lamb-like learn the secret of the Lion.

These follow the Lamb wherever He goes.

Hi sequuntur Agnum quocumque ierit,
Hi empti sunt. Again. They were purchased. Were carried off.

Hi empti sunt ex hominibus,

These were carried off from men,
(From among men, from the presence of men),

primitiae Deo, et Agno,

first-fruits to God, and to the Lamb:

et in ore eorum non est inventum mendacium,

and in their mouth,
and on their lips no lie was found;

(The lie of man, the adult lie, the earthly lie.
The soiled lie.
The dirty lie).
sine macula enim sunt ante thronum Dei,

They are without spot before the throne of God.[7]

I believe that a good argument can be made, from the writings of Péguy and Thérèse and Chesterton, that, like the Holy Innocents of Bethlehem, the myriad children slaughtered each year by abortion die as victims of an anti-Christian, anti-Christ culture of death, killed by the spiritual successors of Herod. Drawing on the teaching of Pope St Leo the Great quoted above, one might then conclude that, by analogy with the Innocents of the first Year of the Lord, the Innocents of the twentieth century *anno Domini* have also died as martyrs in the strict sense. Through the very fact of their infancy,

which Herod and the powers of Hell so hate, they have confessed
the divine Word incarnate, and so, by a Baptism of blood, Christ's
grace of justification has been communicated to them: the guilt of
original sin has been remitted, their souls have been sanctified
inwardly, and the gates of Heaven opened up to them.

This is only a speculation. However, there seems to be some
support for at least some elements of the argument in Pope John
Paul II's encyclical *Evangelium Vitae*. There the Holy Father says that
the Child whom the Dragon seeks to devour in the vision of St John
(cf. Rev. 12:4) is 'a figure of Christ' and at the same time 'a figure of
every person, every child, especially every helpless baby whose life is
threatened, because, as the Council reminds us, 'by his Incarnation
the Son of God has united Himself in some fashion with every man'.
It is precisely in the 'flesh' of every man that Christ continues to
reveal himself and to enter into fellowship with us, *so that rejection of
human life, in whatever form that rejection takes, is really a rejection of
Christ.* This is the fascinating but also demanding truth which Christ
reveals to us, and which his Church continues untiringly to
proclaim: 'Whoever receives one such child in my name receives
me' (Matt. 18:5); 'Truly, I say to you, as you did it to one of the least
of these my brethren, you did it to me' (Matt. 25:40).[8]

Notes

[1] 'Le mystère des saints innocents', *Oeuvres poétiques complètes* (Paris
     1954), p. 820.
[2] Ibid., 819.
[3] *In Epiphaniae solemnitate sermo* 2, n. 3; *Sources Chrétiennes* 22B, p. 224.
[4] 'Le mystère des saints innocents', op. cit., p. 823.
[5] '... l'ultimo è tutto d'Angelici ludi' (Dante, *Paradiso*, Canto 28, 126).
[6] Preaching on the feast of St Stephen, St Bonaventure says: 'Grace is an
     influence calling the soul back to its first simplicity. Now the simpler
     something is, the stronger (*virtuosius*) it is, and the stronger it is, the
     braver it is. Therefore, since Stephen was full of grace, he was full of
     fortitude' (*De Sancto Stephano martyr sermo* 1, 2; *Sancti Bonaventurae
     opera omnia*, vol. 9 [Quaracchi: Typographia Collegii S. Bonaventurae,
     1901], p. 480).
[7] 'Le mystère des saints innocents', op. cit., p. 806f.
[8] *Evangelium Vitae*, n. 104. The passage in italics is partly italicized in the
     original text.
[*] The Editor and publishers are gratefuly for permission granted by
     T. & T. Clark to re-print this section of J. Saward, *The Way of the Lamb.
     The Spirit of Childhood and the End of the Age* (Edinburgh: T. & T. Clark,
     1999).

10

An appeal to the Church: the Agreed Statement of the Solesmes Consultation, and some supplementary theses

The Agreed Statement

Given the morally unanimous opinion of the Fathers of the Church, of St Thomas Aquinas, of the teaching of the ordinary Magisterium and of the witness of the Sacred Liturgy that infants can be martyrs, and that the Baptism of blood avails for justification, the Church can declare in individual cases, based on reliable testimony, that infants, even unborn, who are killed on account of an explicit hatred of the Christian faith or of the other virtues of the Christian life are in fact holy martyrs and may be invoked and venerated as such by all the faithful. This martyrdom can be declared only in cases in which the animation of the foetus by the rational soul is beyond all doubt (for example: after the first trimester). *Nota bene: The last statement in this paragraph simply recognises that the Catholic Church has made no definitive judgment about the moment when the soul is infused into the human foetus. In no way does it imply that the signatories are calling in question the certain and grave immorality of direct abortion from the moment of biological conception onwards. They fully accept the teaching of John Paul II on this point: 'From the standpoint of moral obligation, the mere probability that we are dealing with a person is enough to justify the most unequivocal prohibition of any intervention which seeks to eliminate a human embryo' (Encyclical Letter Evangelium Vitae, No. 60).*

Such a declaration would be a new and organic development of doctrine on the practical level drawn from two facts: that the Church venerates some infants as martyrs, and that she venerates some adult martyrs who died without Baptism or circumcision.

The Very Revd. Hugh Barbour, O. Praem., Prior, St Michael's Abbey, Orange, California, USA.

The Revd. Professor Denis Biju-Duval, Pontifical Lateran University, Rome.

The Revd. Professor Francis Frost, Foyer Sacerdotal International, Ars, France.

The Revd. Professor Brian Harrison, O.S., Pontifical Catholic University of Puerto Rico.

The Revd. Aidan Nichols, O.P., Prior, Blackfriars, Cambridge, England.

Dr Michele M. Schumacher, University of Fribourg, Switzerland.

The supplementary theses for further study and reflection

1. Can the unborn become martyrs also because of an *implicit odium fidei* or *odium Christi* on the part of at least one of those responsible for their death? In the light of Pope John Paul II's exposition of the Gospels to the effect that 'the rejection of human life, in its various forms, is really the rejection of Christ' (*Evangelium Vitae*, no. 104), and given that direct abortion is always or nearly always the deliberate and unqualified rejection of a life recognized to be (at least potentially) both human and totally innocent, are we not entitled to say that in every, or almost every, direct killing of an unborn human person – a person, that is, who, we can know, is not in mortal sin at the time of death – there is an at least implicit hatred of Christ, or of the fifth commandment, which renders that infant's death a case of martyrdom and Baptism of blood? (Harrison)

2. *Evangelium Vitae* no. 58 gives us the elements which make of abortion an especially grave crime:

   i   The absolute innocence of the victim.
   ii His weakness, which deprives him of every means of defence and even of complaint.
   iii Finally, the fact that the child is totally entrusted to the care of his mother and society, since he is absolutely incapable of taking responsibility for himself.

   The little child in his mother's womb is thus an icon of the poor – the person who disposes of nothing by himself, and can only entrust himself to God for what concerns the value of his life, and to men for what concerns his protection and growth (in the same way as elderly people at the end of their lives, and the severely handicapped).

This absolute poverty of the child in his mother's womb makes of him a being particularly vulnerable to the powers of evil, to the reign of sin and death (cf. Rom. 5:12ff.). When abortion reaches him, he is the very image of man as heir to Adam, here and now wounded and vulnerable to the owners of evil without ever having participated personally therein.

Now St Paul tells us that, where sin abounded, grace abounded all the more (cf. Rom. 5:17). In other words, since the victory of Christ over sin and death, it is impossible that any man should remain the sheer victim of evil, and without the possibility of being saved. That is why *Gaudium et Spes* 22 teaches that 'the Holy Spirit in a manner known only to God offers to every man the possibility of being associated with the Paschal Mystery'. If the infant slain in its mother's womb is *par excellence* the poor one among the poor, the sheer victim of sin and death, then by the evangelical logic of the love of preference of Jesus for the littlest ones, he must also be in a privileged position with regard to what touches salvation and victory.

This 'privilege' in the order of grace for child victims of abortion – just because it is a privilege – cannot be fully defined from the viewpoint of revelation.

- It may be that they enter into eternal glory with the title of martyrs, baptized in the Blood of Christ. Indeed, just as Christ is not enclosed within [limited by] his sacraments, so he is not enclosed within [limited by] the canonical definition which the Church furnishes for the title of martyr (and for Baptism of blood).
- It may also be that this privilege involves 'offering the possibility of being associated with the Paschal Mystery' by an act of freedom – since, after all, Christ gave a human assent to his Father from his Mother's womb. That is a privilege because it makes of the child not only a beneficiary of Christ's victory, but also a participant therein. But such an act of freedom opens the possibility of saying 'no' (just as it does for us). (Biju-Duval)

3   The granting of salvation to the murdered child who has made no motion *ex parte eius* represents the love of Christ on the Cross perfectly by magnifying and glorifying the gratuitousness

of divine Love, which does not need the creature to act first.
(Kwasnieski)

4   The proposal that aborted children should be officially recog-
    nised by the Magisterium as martyrs can be seen as a new explicit
    perception of what is implicitly contained in the deposit of faith,
    when it is situated in the context of the ecclesiology of the
    Second Vatican Council, according to which the Church is a
    universal sacrament of salvation. Two affirmations are particu-
    larly important for giving foundation to this perception:

    i   the intimate association of the sponsal Church with the
         universal outreach of the redemptive act of her Head;
    ii   the spiritual maternity of Mary which only comes to full
         fruition through the exercise by the Church, as Spouse of
         Jesus, of her own maternity. (Frost)

5   In virtue of his innocent suffering, the aborted child shares in
    the power of Christ's absolutely unique Sacrifice to open the
    door of consciences to the action of the Holy Spirit whose
    'convincing concerning sin' (cf. John 16:8–9) – i.e. in refer-
    ence to the Cross), enables the conversion whereby one is open
    to the gift of forgiveness. (Schumacher)

6   It is the sole prerogative of the Pope and of the universal
    Magisterium to examine the evidence and to determine
    whether or not aborted babies can be claimed as members of
    the Church. In the absence of such a determination, the faith-
    ful may not presume this, but can only hope and pray,
    reassured that in the end, whichever be the case, 'God shall
    wipe away every tear from their eyes, and death shall be no
    more, nor mourning, nor crying, nor sorrow shall be any more,
    for the former things are passed away' (Rev. 21:4). (McCarthy)

A postscript to the Agreed Statement and supplementary theses

Philippe Jobert, O.S.B.

The whole argument of this cause is founded on the basis of the universality of the salvific will of God. It implies two main considerations:

1. Salvation is considered in its principle, which is the mercy of God and the justification Christ brings about on the Cross: this is God's work.
2. This work of God has, consequently, no limits. It is intrinsically universal, offered to all. The limits come only from human beings who resist the salvific power of the blood of Christ.

It is in the light of this universal salvific power that the case of unborn children has to be considered. Not having the use of their free will, they do not resist or limit the effects of the universality of Christ's power to save. For his part, Christ does everything to suppress the power of sin, which he defeated on the Cross. His victory over original sin is absolute and definitive. His triumph over death, fulfilled in the Resurrection, is initiated in these children at the moment of their own violent deaths by the gift of grace – the resurrection of souls. The issue for the children of Christ's saving work is the glorification of God's mercy on account of Christ alone, since nothing in their redemption can be related to human co-operation.

The same reasoning should be invoked in connexion with the *martyrdom* of unborn children. Martyrdom is a grace from God, so given to some who co-operate by the engagement of their freedom as to become at the same time a personal act expressive of supreme charity. In the children's case, since they lack the use of their freedom, the question of personal co-operation does not arise. This martyrdom is exclusively the gratuitous gift of Christ, giving himself as King of martyrs in order to continue, through all these unborn ones, his witness to divine truth. There is no place here for exceptions, neither from Christ's side nor from that of the children, who conform to his likeness in a death for the truth about life. This martyrdom is inherently universal, a participation of all [aborted] children in the martyrdom of Christ.

So essential is this universality of salvation and martyrdom in the case of [aborted] unborn children that to seek out an individual case of martyrdom in some child killed through abortion *in odium fidei* would completely miss the point. For in such a case, the universal salvific will of God and the martyrdom of Christ are not taken into account. The charism of martyrdom is reduced to the human level, and the exceptional human circumstances of the death of one person only. The glory of martyrdom would accrue to this person, not to the mercy of God and Christ crucified.

In interpreting the Gospel revelation of the universally salvific divine will, a continuing tradition moves from St Augustine, through the Second Council of Orange and the Council of Trent, enlarging all the while on a restricted number of the predestined by reference to a wider and more merciful teaching of the Church. To meet the case of [aborted] unborn children the Church would need to take a step in this direction. The same can be said for the definition of martyrdom. But all this in keeping with the traditional lines of development of Christian doctrine.

Appendix: Sources in the Magisterium and St Thomas

John F. McCarthy

In what follows, some further discussion is provided of relevant Church pronouncements and (especially) of texts from the writings of St Thomas Aquinas, the classical theologian of the Latin Church.

From the teaching of the Magisterium

The rights of a human fetus

With regard to the claiming of aborted babies by the Church, one factor is the increased awareness in the Church of our time of the fully human status of infants in the womb from the first moment of conception, a fact that was not clearly recognized in earlier times. The *Catechism of the Catholic Church* has this to say (no. 2270): 'Human life must be respected and protected absolutely from the first moment of conception. From the first moment of his existence, a human being must be recognized as having the rights of a person – among which is the inviolable right of every innocent being to life.' Although the evil of abortion from the first moment of conception has always been condemned by the Church, based on the common realization that from the moment of fertilization this new living thing is dynamically ordered to becoming a human person, we are now certain that from the moment of fertilization this new living thing *is* a human person, whose human soul has been directly created by God (*CCC*, no. 366), and who thus is already endowed with a human intellect and a human will, even though he cannot use these (apart from preternatural assistance from God) until a sufficient organic base has been built up. This fact of pervasive human existence provides added motivation for the

Church to extend her maternal care to infants in the womb. In spite of this awareness, worldly society has unfortunately moved toward 'legalizing' abortion and has found the means to make abortions ever more convenient and available. This gives the Church added reason to be concerned about the fate of aborted children. We have, then, in the Church increased concern for all babies whose lives are threatened in the womb and increased awareness of the social responsibility resulting from the phenomenon of abortion.

The necessity of Baptism

The Church gives witness to the truth revealed by Jesus that 'unless a man be born again of water and the Holy Spirit, he cannot enter into the kingdom of God' (John 3:5). How does the Church interpret these words? The *Catechism of the Catholic Church* relates them to the words of Jesus in Mark 16:16, where he says: 'He that believes and is baptized shall be saved; but he that believes not shall be condemned' – and it declares: 'Baptism is necessary for salvation for those to whom the Gospel has been proclaimed and who have had the possibility of asking for this sacrament', so that 'God has bound salvation to the sacrament of Baptism, but he himself is not bound by his sacraments' (*CCC*, no. 1257). Thus, the Church allows for the salvation of some apart from Baptism of water. 'The Church has always held the firm conviction that those who suffer death for the sake of the faith without having received Baptism are baptized by their death for and with Christ. This *Baptism of blood*, like the *desire for Baptism*, brings about the fruits of Baptism without being a sacrament' (*CCC*, no. 1258). Furthermore, 'Since Christ died for all, and since all men are in fact called to one and the same destiny, which is divine, we must hold that the Holy Spirit offers to all the possibility of being made partakers, in a way known to God, of the Paschal mystery' (*Gaudium et Spes*, 22, §5). Hence, 'Every man who is ignorant of the Gospel of Christ and of his Church, but seeks the truth and does the will of God in accordance with his understanding of it, can be saved. It may be supposed that such persons would have *desired Baptism explicitly* if they had known its necessity' (*CCC*, no. 1260). Two facts about aborted babies are to be noted in the light of these quotations:

a) aborted babies have had no possibility whatsoever to know about the Gospel of Christ and of his Church, but have sought the truth in the one way that was open to them, which was to grow physically in the womb;

b) they have suffered a violent death at the hands of persons acting contrary to the teaching of Christ and of the Church.

Children who die without Baptism of water

As I pointed out in my article (*vide supra*, Chapter 2), the Limbo of Children is not an official doctrine of the Church. 'The Church has never made any official pronouncement on the reality or nature of limbo; but it does teach that baptism in some form is required for salvation.'[1] The *Catechism of the Catholic Church* leans toward the salvation of such children, when it says (no. 1261): 'As regards *children who have died without Baptism*, the Church can only entrust them to the mercy of God, as she does in her funeral rites for them. Indeed, the great mercy of God, "who wants all men to be saved" (1 Tim. 2:4),[2] and Jesus' tenderness toward children which caused him to say: "Let the children come to me, do not hinder them" (Mark 10:14), allow us to hope that there is a way of salvation for children who have died without Baptism', that is, without Baptism of water. The *Catechism* is here reechoing the words of *Lumen Gentium* (no. 22):

> Those who, through no fault of their own, do not know the Gospel of Christ or of his Church, but who, nevertheless, seek God with a sincere heart, and, moved by grace, try in their actions to do his will as they know it through the dictates of their conscience – those too may achieve eternal salvation. Nor shall divine Providence deny the assistance necessary for salvation to those who, without any fault of theirs, have not yet arrived at an explicit knowledge of God, and who, not without grace, strive to lead a good life.

The opening prayer of the funeral Mass of a child who died before Baptism says rather cautiously: 'Lord, listen to the prayers of this family that has faith in you. In their sorrow at the death of this child, may they find hope in your infinite mercy.' There is here no mention of eternal beatitude in Heaven, but there *is* a mention of the Christian faith and Christian hope of others in relation to the deceased child. The point I am making here is that, if there may be a way of salvation for children in general who have died without Baptism, how much more may there be a way of salvation for children who have been killed before they could have made any act of the will that might hinder their call to Heaven. Through no fault of their own they had not yet arrived at an explicit knowledge of

God, and they were striving in the only way open to them to lead a good life. The context of their violent death could be for them an instrument of grace, allowing the Church to be more explicit about their salvation, although it is the sole prerogative of the Magisterium of the Church to determine whether this be so.

In a fifth-century response to the heresy of Pelagianism, the Sixteenth Provincial Council of Carthage (418), guided by St Augustine, who was present as a member, in a canon which was not afterwards included among the articles of faith binding on the universal Church,[3] declared as follows:

It has likewise been decided that if anyone says that for this reason the Lord said, 'In my Father's house there are many mansions' (John 14:2), [namely] that it might be understood that in the kingdom of Heaven there will be some middle place or some place anywhere where the blessed infants live who have departed from this life without Baptism, in the absence of which they cannot enter into the kingdom of Heaven, which is life eternal, let him be anathema. For, when the Lord says: 'Unless a man be born again of water and the Holy Spirit, he shall not enter into the kingdom of God' (John 3:5), what Catholic will doubt that whoever has not deserved to be a coheir of Christ will be a partner of the Devil? For whoever is missing on the right hand must without doubt be present on the left (DH 224).

Pope Pius VI, in the Apostolic Constitution *Auctorem fidei* (1794), promulgated in opposition to the Synod of Pistoia (1786), censured as

false, rash, and injurious to Catholic schools ... the doctrine which rejects as a Pelagian fable that place in the lower regions which the faithful generally designate by the name of the Limbo of Children, in which the souls of those dying with original sin alone are punished with the punishment of damnation but without the penalty of fire, as if by the very fact of removing the punishment of fire they were introducing that intermediate place and state free of guilt and penalty between the kingdom of God and eternal damnation about which Pelagians idly talk (DH 2626).

The Second Ecumenical Council of Lyons (1274) had already declared that 'the souls of those who die in actual mortal sin or only in original sin descend forthwith into the Inferno, but to undergo different punishments' (DH 858; cf. DH 1306). The Ecumenical Council of Florence (1442) decreed: 'But regarding children, on account of the often occurring danger of death: since they cannot be helped by another remedy except by the sacrament of Baptism, through which they are snatched from the power of the Devil and adopted as children of God, [the Holy Roman Church] advises that holy Baptism ought not to be deferred ...' (DH 1349). In view of this magisterial teaching on the necessity of Baptism for salvation, broaching the question of aborted babies in particular must mean considering whether they might be saved through a vicarious desire for the sacrament of Baptism (as I suggested in the body of my article under the theme of the prayer of the Church) or through Baptism of blood in association with the Passion and Death of Jesus (as I also suggested in a comparison with the Holy Innocents of Bethlehem). Thus, it is not my aim to question the existence of the Limbo of Children, or to deny that those who die only in original sin will be taken there, but rather to examine whether aborted children may be sanctified at the moment of their death and thus not die in the state of original sin.

In 1546 the Ecumenical Council of Trent pronounced that 'if anyone denies that infants newly born from their mothers' wombs are to be baptized ..., or says ... that they derive nothing of original sin from Adam which must be expiated by the laver of regeneration', let him be anathema (DH 1514). In 1547 the Council of Trent went on to declare that this transfer to the state of grace 'after the promulgation of the Gospel cannot be effected except through the laver of regeneration or through a desire for it (*aut eius voto*)' (DH 1524). These declarations affirm that infants incur original sin at their conception and that they cannot be transferred to the state of sanctifying grace without Baptism of water or of desire. In the present study we are examining whether aborted infants might be sanctified by something equivalent to Baptism of desire at the moment of their death. We are not so much questioning whether some deceased children go to the Limbo of Children as we are suggesting that aborted children do not go there.

Pope Pius XII touched on this matter when he wrote: 'Under the present economy there is no other way of giving this [supernatural] life to the child who is still without the use of reason ... In the case of a grown-up person, an act of love may suffice for obtaining sanctifying grace and making up for the lack of Baptism. To the child still unborn or the child just born this path is not open.'[4] Pope Pius XII is here proposing that, 'under the present economy' of the visible Church, infants are unable of themselves to supply for the lack of the sacrament of Baptism, but he is not denying that they could be sanctified in some way outside of this economy by a direct intervention of divine grace or through Baptism of blood.

St Alphonsus Liguori[5] defines Baptism of blood as 'the shedding of blood, or death undergone for the faith or for another Christian virtue', and he explains that it remits faults and punishment 'from a kind of privilege based upon an imitation of the Passion of Christ'. He goes on to say that 'martyrdom avails infants as well, seeing that the Church venerates the Holy Innocents as true martyrs.' He adds that 'in adults an acceptance, at least habitual, of martyrdom for a supernatural reason is required': not, therefore, in infants. Thus, if 'the Church knows no other way apart from Baptism [of water] of ensuring children's entry into eternal happiness,[6] this does not mean that the teaching of the Church *excludes* the salvation of children by any other way. Similarly, when the *Roman Catechism* teaches[7] that 'infant children have no other means of salvation except Baptism (of water)', it means that they have no other *ordinary* means by which the Church can ensure their salvation. Thus, there is every reason to insist on the Baptism of infants at the earliest reasonable moment after their birth.

The growth of devotion to the Hearts of Jesus and Mary has made ever more vivid our understanding of the merciful love of Jesus and the maternal love of Mary, the new Eve, for all children coming into this world. This development is embodied in the teaching of the Second Ecumenical Council of the Vatican: 'By her maternal charity, she cares for the brethren of her Son who still journey on earth surrounded by dangers and difficulties, until they are led into their blessed home. Therefore, the Blessed Virgin is invoked in the Church under the titles of Advocate, Helper, Benefactress, and Mediatrix' (*Lumen Gentium*, no. 62). 'The Son whom she brought forth is he whom God placed as the firstborn among many brethren (Rom. 8:29), that is, the faithful, in whose generation and formation she cooperates with a mother's love' (*Lumen Gentium*, no. 63). Infants in the womb about to be aborted are surrounded by dangers and difficulties of the greatest kind. Are we to suppose that Mary, in her superabundant mother's love for the faithful, in whose generation and formation she cooperates, is not concerned about the loss of Heaven threatening infants being aborted? Are we to assume that she is not an advocate, helper, benefactress, or mediatrix for them in their fundamental vocation to eternal life with Jesus in Heaven?

Victory over Satan

When the *Catechism of the Catholic Church* proclaims the inviolate right to life of every infant in the womb (no. 2270), it cites the words of the Lord to the prophet Jeremiah: 'Before I formed you in the womb I knew you, and before you were born I consecrated you' (Jer 1:5). While there is no doubt that the sanctification of an infant living in the womb is in itself a rare and extraordinary grace, nevertheless, a special case can be made for infants facing the moment of their violent death in the womb, in the sense that the grace of sanctification might be expected as a common divine intervention given from the merits of Jesus Christ through the maternal intercession of Mary. The *Catechism*, in explaining the constant petition of the Church to God the Father to 'deliver us from evil' (Matt. 6:13), speaks as follows: 'In this petition, evil is not an abstraction, but refers to a person, Satan, the Evil One, the angel who opposes God' (*CCC*, no. 2851). 'Victory over the "prince of this world" (John 14:30) was won once for all at the Hour when Jesus freely gave himself up to death to give us his life. This is the Judgment of this world, and the prince of this world is "cast out" (John 12:31; Rev. 12:10). "He pursued the woman" (Rev. 12:13–16), but had no hold on her: the new Eve, "full of grace" of the Holy Spirit, is preserved from sin and the corruption of death (the Immaculate Conception and the Assumption of the Most Holy Mother of God, Mary, ever virgin). "Then the dragon was angry with the woman, and went off to make war on the rest of her offspring" (Rev. 12:17). Therefore the Spirit and the Church pray: "Come, Lord Jesus", since his coming will deliver us from the Evil One' (*CCC*, no. 2853). Since the Church prays to Jesus and believes that 'his coming will deliver us from the Evil One', is it not likely that Jesus *does* come to deliver these infants from the original sin by which they are bound to the power of Satan and to offer them the grace of Heaven?

From the teaching of St Thomas Aquinas

The Limbo of Children

The Greek and Latin Fathers of the first four centuries saw in general no more severe penalty for infants who died without Baptism than exclusion from the beatific vision. But St Augustine and the other African Fathers, in opposition to the Pelagians who were holding that infants have no sin, maintained that infants who die in original sin only will still share in the positive misery of the damned, although with a penalty mild enough that they would want to continue in existence. This opinion remained dominant from the fifth to the thirteenth century; a few theologians differed, but St Thomas was the first great theologian to eliminate the pain of suffering from Limbo by reasoning that infants who die in original sin only will live in perfect natural happiness, having lost the blessing of the beatific vision, but with no awareness of having lost it,[8] and this is what the majority of Catholic theologians have continued to hold ever since then.[9] However, it is important to note that St Thomas, in presenting his argument for a Limbo of Children, does not speak about children who die without the sacrament of Baptism, but only of children who die 'in original sin', and it seems obvious that, to the extent that a child might die in the state of original sin, this is a benevolent and convincing solution. But the question before us is whether aborted infants *do* die in the state of original sin.

A way into this issue might take its starting point from a text where St Thomas teaches[10] that all human beings will rise again. 'The resurrection is necessary in order that those who rise again may receive punishment or reward according to their merits. Now either punishment or reward is due to all, either for their own merits, as to adults, or for others' merits, as to children. Therefore, all will rise again.' Daniel 12:2 declares: 'Many of those who sleep in the dust of the earth shall awake.' Does this imply that not all will awake? St Thomas answers: 'Augustine[11] explains *many* as meaning *all*: in fact, this way of speaking is often met with in Holy Writ. Or else the restriction may refer to children condemned (to Limbo) (*quantum ad pueros damnatos*), who, although they shall rise again, are not properly said to awake, since they will have no sense either of pain or of glory, and waking is the unchaining of the senses.' Yet it could be objected that babies who die in their mothers' wombs can never be born again, and so they will not rise again. St Thomas replies:

> We are born again by the grace of Christ that is given to us, but we rise again by the grace of Christ whereby it came about that he took our nature, since it is by this that we are conformed to him in natural things. Hence, those who die in their mother's womb, although they are not born again by receiving grace, will nevertheless rise again on account of the conformity of their nature with him, which conformity they acquired by attaining to the perfection of the human species.

From these quotations we see that St Thomas does visualize little children, and even those who die in the womb, as condemned to the loss of Heaven, and he states that children who die in the womb 'are not born again by receiving grace'. The direction that St Thomas takes in these statements is significant. Whereas he begins with the principle that everyone should receive punishment or reward according to his merits, and children according to the merits of others, he reaches his conclusions on the punishment of little children from the demerits of Adam, rather than arguing to the reward of little children because of the merits of Christ. It was the strongly pessimistic theological tradition of St Thomas's time that seems to have disposed him to take for granted that aborted children die in original sin, but the outlook of today is far more positive and open to the hope of their salvation. And what St Thomas says in the citations that will be given below seems to provide a foundation for the belief that aborted babies are granted the grace of salvation.

The necessity of Baptism

St Thomas teaches that 'sacraments are necessary for human salvation' even though 'the Passion of Christ is a sufficient cause of [that] salvation', because '[sacraments] work in virtue of the Passion of Christ, and the Passion of Christ is in some way applied to men through sacraments, according to what the Apostle says in Rom. 6:3: "…. all we who have been baptized in Christ Jesus have been baptized in his death."'[12] Now 'the power of Christ is linked to us through faith, but the power to remit sins pertains in a special way to his Passion, and so, men are freed from sins especially through faith in his Passion'.[13] Children too need the grace of Baptism: 'That children contract original sin from the sin of Adam is evident from the fact that they are subject to death … And so all the more can children receive grace through Christ that they may reign in eternal life. But the Lord himself says in John 3:15: "Unless one has been born again of water and the Holy Spirit, he cannot enter into the kingdom of God." Consequently, it became necessary to baptize children, in order that, just as through Adam they have incurred damnation in being born, so through Christ they may reach salvation in being reborn.'[14] In sum, 'Baptism of water takes effect from the Passion of Christ, to whom someone is configured through Baptism and, further, from the Holy Spirit, as from the first cause.'

Again: 'The Passion of Christ is shared for a remedy with every baptized person as if that person had suffered and died.'[15] And 'by the Passion of Christ, the door of the heavenly kingdom has been opened for us.'[16] Now,

> although the effect depends upon the first cause, nevertheless the cause exceeds the effect and does not depend upon the effect. And, therefore, besides Baptism of water, one can attain to the effect of the sacrament from the Passion of Christ, inasmuch as one is conformed to him by suffering for Christ.... For the same reason also someone can receive the effect of Baptism by the power of the Holy Spirit, not only without Baptism of water, but also without Baptism of blood, insofar as one's heart is moved by the Holy Spirit to believing and loving God and to repenting of one's sins; whence this is also called Baptism of repentance' (cf. Is. 4:4).

Thus, there are three Baptisms, namely, 'of water, of blood, and of the Spirit (*flaminis*), that is, of the Holy Spirit'.[17] St Augustine is in agreement:

> Whence Augustine says[18]: 'That suffering sometimes fills the place of Baptism, Blessed Cyprian not lightly cites the case of that unbaptized thief to whom it was said, *Today you will be with me in Paradise.* And considering this again and again, I find that not only suffering for the name of Christ can supply what was lacking to Baptism, but also faith and conversion of heart, if perchance, due to the lack of time, a celebration of the mystery of Baptism cannot be arranged.'[19]

With these three kinds of Baptism in mind, St Thomas affirms the necessity of Baptism for salvation: 'Baptism is given for this that someone, having been regenerated by it, may be incorporated into Christ and made a member of him: whence it is said in Galatians 3:27: "For as many of you as have been baptized in Christ have put on Christ." And from this it is manifest that all men are held to Baptism and that without it there cannot be salvation for men.'[20]

Baptism of blood and of desire

Baptism of blood is no contradiction in terms. 'From the side of Christ flowed water for washing and blood for redeeming. Therefore, blood fits the sacrament of the Eucharist, while water fits the sacrament of Baptism. But Baptism has its washing power

from the power of the Blood of Christ.'[21] In fact, Baptism of blood
is even more powerful than Baptism of water.

> For the Passion of Christ works, indeed, in Baptism of water
> by a certain figurative representation; and in Baptism of the
> Spirit, or of repentance, by a certain affection; but in Baptism
> of blood by an imitation of the deed [of Christ on the Cross].
> Similarly, the power of the Holy Spirit works in Baptism of
> water by a certain hidden power, and in Baptism of repen-
> tance by a movement of the heart, but in Baptism of blood by
> a very strong fervour of love and affection (cf. John 15:13).[22]

But Baptism of desire is also possible.

> The sacrament of Baptism can be lacking to someone in fact
> but not in desire, as when someone desires to be baptized, but
> perchance is taken by death before he can receive Baptism.
> Such a one can attain to salvation without actual Baptism on
> account of a desire for Baptism which proceeds from faith
> working through love (Gal. 5:6), through which God, whose
> power is not bound by visible sacraments, interiorly sanctifies
> the man.[23]

Now, according to John 3:5, 'unless a man be born again of water
and the Holy Spirit, he cannot enter into the kingdom of God.'
To this St Thomas replies: 'He who desires to be regenerated
through Baptism of water and the Holy Spirit is regenerated in
heart, although not in body.'[24] Thus, 'The sacrament of Baptism
is said to be necessary for salvation because there cannot be salvation for a man unless he has it at least in wish: which with God is
considered as accomplished.'[25] And so, 'Just as the fathers of old
were saved by faith in Christ to come, so also are we saved by faith
in Christ already having been born and having suffered.'[26] By
Baptism a person is incorporated into Christ as a member of
him.[27] But do not adult converts have to be already believing in
Christ before Baptism will be ministered to them? 'Adults who
believe in Christ beforehand are incorporated into him mentally,
and afterwards, when they are baptized, they are somehow incorporated into him bodily, viz., through a visible sacrament, without
the intention of which they could not have been incorporated
even mentally.'[28]

It may seem to some that for little babies Baptism of blood does
not take the place of Baptism of water, if Baptism of water takes

effect *ex opere operato*, while Baptism of blood takes place only *ex opere operantis*, and, therefore, only with the exercise of charity (cf. 1 Cor. 13), something of which little babies are incapable because they do not have the use of free will. To this problem St Thomas responds as follows: 'Baptism of water takes effect from the Passion of Christ inasmuch as it represents it sacramentally, while Baptism of blood conforms in reality to the Passion of Christ, not by sacramental representation ... [Hence], as regards the *res tantum*, [sanctifying grace], it totally takes the place of Baptism of water, when a moment of need excludes the sacrament.' and so, 'Baptism of blood does not have its effect only *ex opere operantis*, ... but it has it from imitation of the Passion of Christ. So it is said in Apocalypse 7:14 regarding martyrs: "they have washed their garments in the Blood of the Lamb," and, therefore, children, although they do not have free will, if they are killed for Christ, are saved as baptized in his Blood.'[29]

Sacraments before the coming of Christ

St Thomas teaches that there were sacraments before the coming of Christ. 'It was fitting that before the coming of Christ there be certain visible signs by which a man could profess his faith concerning the future coming of the Saviour. And signs of this kind are called sacraments.'[30] The efficient cause, to be sure, cannot come afterwards in time, yet nevertheless,

> the fathers of old were sanctified by faith in the Passion of Christ, as are we. But the sacraments of the Old Law were declarations of that faith inasmuch as they signified the Passion of Christ and its effects. It is thus evident that the sacraments of the Old Law did not have in themselves any operational power of conferring sanctifying grace, but they only signified the faith by which they [the fathers of old] were sanctified.[31]

Hence, 'circumcision conferred grace inasmuch as it was a sign of the future Passion of Christ.'[32]

Circumcision

According to St Thomas, since Abraham was noted for his faith and is called our father in faith, 'a sign (*signaculum*), or sacrament, of faith was fashioned for him, namely, circumcision.'[33] And St

Thomas explains that circumcision had an express likeness to the taking away of original sin in four ways, of which the fourth way is 'with regard to the shedding of blood, in which is signified the Passion of Christ, through which satisfaction would be made for original sin, and, with regard to this benefit, circumcision is defined as the sign (*signaculum*) of healing from original sin.'[34] And so the circumcised were thereby disposed for eternal life, even though the gate of Heaven was not yet open. '... because the final positive effect of grace is to make one worthy of eternal life, which was done through circumcision, as is now done also through Baptism', although 'in Baptism greater grace is given'.[35] In fact, the benefit of circumcision was also more restricted than that of Baptism, 'because it had a determined people, a determined sex, and a determined time [the eighth day of birth], which does not occur in Baptism'.[36] Circumcision signified justification by faith in the coming Passion of Christ, 'in such wise that the man who was receiving circumcision was professing that he accepted this faith, either an adult for himself or another for little children'.[37] So circumcision was like the sacraments of the New Law in that it could wipe away sin by its very performance.

> It is fitting that a sin contracted from another be taken away by another and, therefore, in every stage (*statu*) after the Fall there has been some remedy by which original sin could be taken away in virtue of the Passion of Christ. And, again, because a born baby, before he had the use of free will, was not able to prepare himself for grace, in order that he should not be left without any remedy at all, it was needful that some remedy be given which would wipe out sin by its very performance (*ex opere operato*), and this remedy was circumcision. Therefore, it is conceded by all that, as it signified a removal, it did take away sin, and in this it coincided in some way with the sacraments of the New Law, because it accomplished what it figured.[38]

The role of faith

St Thomas, therefore, points out that, 'before the coming of Christ, people were incorporated into Christ through faith in his future advent, the sign of whose faith was circumcision.' St Paul writes to the Romans:

> Blessed is the man against whom the Lord will not reckon his

sin.' Is this blessing pronounced only upon the circumcised, or also upon the uncircumcised? We say that faith was reckoned to Abraham as righteousness. How then was it reckoned to him? Was it before or after he had been circumcised? It was not after, but before he was circumcised. He received circumcision as a sign or seal of the righteousness which he had by faith while he was still uncircumcised. The purpose was to make him the father of all who believe without being circumcised and who thus have righteousness reckoned to them, and likewise the father of the circumcised who are not merely circumcised but also follow the example of the faith which our father Abraham had before he was circumcised (Rom. 4:8–12 [*RSV*]).

And, opines St Thomas, before circumcision was instituted, as St Gregory confirms[39], people were incorporated into Christ by the offering of sacrifices, by which the ancient fathers professed their faith. 'Also after the coming of Christ, people are incorporated into Christ through faith, according to Ephesians 3:17: "that Christ may dwell in your hearts through faith." ... Hence, although the sacrament itself of Baptism was not always necessary for salvation, nonetheless, faith, of which Baptism is the sacrament, *was* always necessary.'[40]

Justification of children through faith

Before the institution of circumcision, did faith alone suffice for the justification of children? St Thomas replies:

Just as before the institution of circumcision faith in [the] Christ to come justified both children and adults, so also [was that the case] when circumcision had been given .... But it is probable that believing parents said some prayers to God for their newborn infants, and especially for those in danger, or they performed some blessing upon them which was a kind of sign of faith (*signaculum fidei*), just as adults offered prayers and sacrifices for themselves.[41]

However, we do not read in Sacred Scripture that the patriarch Isaac, for instance, offered sacrifice to God. To this St Thomas replies that, while St Gregory (again) maintains[42] that among the ancients original sin was remitted through the offering of sacrifices, nevertheless, 'Isaac signified Christ inasmuch as he was offered in sacrifice (Gen. 22:9–10), and so it was not needful that he should signify as offering sacrifice.'[43] Furthermore, 'it is also said of the children of the ancients that they were saved in the faith of their parents (*in fide parentium*).'[44] But circumcision was prescribed in the Law for the eighth day after birth, not before, and those who were born during the forty years of wandering in the desert were uncircumcised (cf. Josh. 5:5–6). For St Thomas: 'If some died uncircumcised, they were in the same situation as those who died before the institution of circumcision. And this is also to be understood regarding boys who died before their eighth day in the time of the Law.'[45] Moreover, circumcision was incomplete in its extension only to males. St Thomas explains: 'Circumcision was instituted as a sign of the faith of Abraham, who believed that he would be the father of the Christ promised to him (Rom. 4:11 ff.), and, therefore, it suitably pertained only to males.'[46]

Faith in the mediator

St Thomas asks 'whether faith alone availed little children for the remission of original sin, seeing that Gregory says that for little children faith alone, for adults sacrifices and offerings, were effective [among the ancients].[47] And St Thomas responds to his own question: 'Faith in the Mediator was always effective for healing from original sin: their own in those who had the use of free will; of another in the others, lest a divine remedy should be entirely lacking to them.'[48] It seems to St Thomas, following the teaching of St Gregory the Great,

> for little children faith alone sufficed without any exterior sign [before the institution of Baptism]; not, however, the habit alone of faith, but an act of it regarding the salvation of this child, by force of an interior profession of faith, whosoever it might be who referred a profession of faith to this child; but this pertained more to his parents, who were obliged to take care of the child and through whom he had contracted original sin.[49]

How could faith alone suffice for the salvation of a child? 'In as much as at one time the faith of another together with some witnessing sufficed for the salvation of a child, this was so insofar as that witnessing had the sacramental power which Baptism of water has now.'[50]

Baptism of babies

In comparing the plight of babies before the institution of Baptism with that of babies in the New Testament, St Thomas treats the following problem: 'The age of childhood is more inclining towards pity than is mature age ... But children are not forgiven original sin simply in exchange for the faith and contrition of others, if Baptism of water be not administered to them. It seems, therefore, that original [sin] together with actual sin is not remitted to adults either without Baptism of water.'[51] And he answers thus: 'Since the salvation of a man regards the greatest values, it cannot be taken away from someone who wants it. But it is in the power of a man to impede another man from being baptized with water. Therefore, there can be salvation even without Baptism of water by faith and contrition alone.'[52] St Thomas points out that Baptism of penance, that is, of desire, is not ordinarily sufficient for salvation, but it is sufficient 'when the moment of need excludes the sacrament from being received, for then, although the repentance is without Baptism in act, it is, nevertheless, with the desire and intention of Baptism, and the wish is considered as the accomplished fact for him who does not have time to perform it'.[53] And so, 'although the age of children is more pitiful, it is, nonetheless, needful, if they must be saved, that there be some reason for salvation in them. And because they cannot be saved by their own act of free will, it is needful that they be saved through the sacrament of Baptism.'[54] But as regards the infant children of non-believers, St Thomas is of the opinion that to baptize them against the will of their parents, even to rescue a child in danger of physical death from the danger of eternal death, would be 'contrary to natural justice' and an infringement upon the order of the natural law 'in virtue of which a child is under the care of his father'.[55]

Sanctification without the sacraments

St Thomas points out that 'it is Christ who principally baptizes' (cf. John 1:33)[56] And so: 'The man who baptizes exercises only an external ministry, while it is Christ who baptizes internally, and he can use all men for whatever he wants.'[57] The human person baptizing acts 'as a minister of Christ, who does not bind [i.e. limit] his power to baptized persons or to the sacraments'.[58] Thus Christ, without the sacrament of Penance, conferred the effect of the sacrament upon Magdalen (Luke 7:48).[59] And Christ conferred Baptism of blood upon the Good Thief on Calvary,

even though he was not put to death for witnessing to the teaching of Christ:

> Nor was that thief crucified for the name of Christ. On the
> contrary, as Jerome says, 'Christ turned a penalty for murder
> into a martyrdom (*Christus homicidii poenam in illo latrone fecit
> esse martyrium*)', and it is to be said that he had something of
> martyrdom, namely, a penalty and a righteous will, and he
> lacked something for martyrdom, namely a cause, just as in
> the [Holy] Innocents there was lacking a righteous will, but
> there was a penalty and a cause.[60]

But God can also administer the sacraments through Angels.

> Just as God did not bind his power to the sacraments in such
> wise that he could not confer the effect of the sacraments
> without the sacraments, so also he did not bind his power to
> the ministers of the Church in such wise that he could not
> bestow even upon angels the power of ministering in sacra-
> mental matters. And, since the good angels are messengers of
> truth, if some sacramental ministry should be carried out by
> good angels, it must be considered valid (*ratum*), because it
> ought to be evident that this was done by divine will, as certain
> churches are said to have been consecrated by angelic
> ministry.[61]

However, 'what men do in a lower way, viz., through sensible sacraments, which are proportionate to their nature, angels do as
higher ministers in a higher way, viz., by invisibly cleansing, illuminating, and perfecting.'[62]

The child in the womb

Regarding babies in the womb: 'Children in their mothers' wombs
. . . cannot be subjected to the actions of humans in such a way that
through their ministry they may receive the sacraments of salvation. But they can be subject to the work of God, in whose presence
they live, that by a privilege of grace they may obtain sanctification,
as is evident from those who have been sanctified in the womb'.[63]
According to St Thomas, 'Sanctification in the womb is Baptism of
the Spirit (*Baptismus flaminis*).'[64]
St Thomas mentions the Blessed Virgin Mary, John the Baptist,
and the prophet Jeremiah as prime examples of persons who have

been sanctified 'outside of the common law as though miraculously in their mothers' wombs'.[65] An act of the mind can extend equally to the born or to the preborn. If, therefore, faith ever were sufficient for wiping out original sin, why cannot those in the womb be cleansed from original sin through the faith of another? St Thomas replies:

> A child living in the womb of his mother does not, as far as human knowledge can tell (*quantum ad humanam cognitionem pertinet*), have being that is separate (*distinctum*) from his mother, and, therefore, cannot be reached by an act of man, whether in these times to be cleansed from original sin through Baptism, or in those [ancient] times to be cleansed through the faith of his parents, but he can be divinely cleansed, as appears in the case of those who have been sanctified in the womb.[66]

Nevertheless, a child in his mother's womb is 'entirely another according to the rational soul which he has from without.'[67] Why, then, such as was the case at Sodom, does God punish little children for the sins of their parents? 'Little children are temporally punished together with their parents for two reasons: because they belong to their parents, and so their parents are punished in them; and because this turns to their good, lest, if they were spared, they might be imitators of their parents' malice and thus might merit heavier penalties.'[68]

Children and the divine mercy

St Thomas maintains that salvation is available in some way to everyone.

> Just as there was no stage of the world at which the way of salvation was shut to the human race, so there is no age of the individual man in which the way of salvation is shut. And so, since original sin is in children, by which they are impeded from attaining to eternal salvation, it is needful that some remedy be used for them to remove the aforesaid impediment, and this is Baptism. Hence, whoever denies that Baptism can be afforded to little children is denying the divine mercy, on account of which it is heretical to say this.[69]

Yet, St Thomas holds that 'no one should be baptized before he is born from the womb', or, more strongly, 'in no way can those living in their mother's womb be baptized.'[70] But those in the womb have independent existence. 'A child living in the mother's womb pertains to her by a certain connection of distinct bodies.'[71] Babies in their mothers' wombs cannot be baptized 'because they cannot be subjected to the activity of the ministers of the Church, through whom such remedies are administered.'[72] As Augustine says in his letter to Dardanus:[73] 'No one is reborn unless he is first born.' And, adds St Thomas, 'Baptism is a spiritual regeneration. Therefore, no one should be baptized before he is born from the womb.'[74] But, he adds, 'if a mother should die while a child is living in her womb, the womb should be opened and the child should be baptized.'[75] Furthermore, he notes, 'Those who are asleep are not to be baptized unless they are in immediate danger of death.'[76] And babies cannot sin gravely either before death or after: 'Since children before the use of reason do not have an inordinate act of the will, neither will they have one after death.'[77]

The salvation of babies

How can babies be baptized, when they cannot intend to be baptized? St Thomas points out that

> as children in their mothers' wombs do not receive nourishment by themselves, but are sustained by the nourishment of their mother, so also children not having the use of reason, being, as it were, in the womb of Mother Church, receive salvation by an act of the Church.... And, for the same reason, they can be said to be intending, not by an act of their own intention, since they sometimes resist and cry, but by the act of those by whom they are being offered.[78]

Can little babies have faith or a good conscience without having the use of reason?

> A little child believes through others, not by himself, and so he is questioned, not himself [directly] but through others, and those questioned confess the faith of the Church in the person of the child, who is aggregated to this faith by the sacrament of faith. But the child acquires a good conscience even in himself, not, to be sure, in act, but in disposition (*habitu*) through sanctifying grace.[79]

In the Church of the Saviour, as Augustine says[80], 'Little children are presented to receive spiritual grace, not so much by those in whose hands they are carried, although also by them, if they too are good believers, as by the entire company of the saints and of the faithful.' And thus St Thomas is led to say in a passage rich with implications: 'the faith of one [person], indeed of the whole Church, benefits the little child through the working of the Holy Spirit, who unites the Church and communicates the good things of one [individual] to another.'[81] In fact, he avers, 'The prayers which are said in the administration of the sacraments are offered to God, not on the part of the individual person, but on the part of the entire Church.'[82] Consequently, 'Children believe, not by their own act, but by the faith of the Church, which is imparted to them. And, by dint of this faith, grace and the virtues are conferred upon them.'[83] Furthermore, 'since children are baptized, not in their own faith but in the faith of the Church, they are all equally disposed towards Baptism, and they all receive an equal effect in Baptism.'[84] Hence, it does not really matter what the intention is of those who are carrying them.[85]

Application to the question of aborted babies

Just as the teaching of the Church allows us 'to hope that there is a way of salvation' for little children who die without having received the sacrament of Baptism, so does the teaching of St Thomas leave the door of salvation open to them. St Thomas does not teach that aborted babies are saved, but what he says in scattered responses relating to this question seems to lay a solid theological foundation for hope of their salvation. Regarding these responses I note the following.

(a) When St Thomas recommends that the babies of non-believers not be baptized, even in danger of death, if their parents are unwilling, he must be speaking only about remote danger of death, because to grant a natural right to parents of excluding their children from Heaven is unthinkable. In fact, it is against the teaching and practice of the Church (cf. canon 868.2 of the 1983 *Code of Canon Law*). And we can confidently say that the natural right of parents to care for their child ends with their decision to murder their child and is then superseded by the right of the Church to sanctify that child (cf. Prov. 24:11).

(b) St Thomas says with reference to the Holy Innocents of

Bethlehem, that they are considered to be martyrs, even though they did not have the conscious intention or desire to suffer for Christ, because they *did* suffer the penalty of death on account of him. Hence, if babies killed in the womb suffer the penalty of death in some way because of Christ, they may be eligible to become martyrs of Christ.

(c) St Thomas declares that little children intend and believe, not by themselves, but through others, namely, through their parents or their sponsors, but especially through the entire membership of the Church. Hence, to the extent that babies being aborted are sponsored in faith by members of the Church in Heaven or on earth, they may be said to have belief in the saving power of Christ and to have the intention of suffering in union with the Passion of Christ, which adds another element to their eligibility for the grace of martyrdom.

(d) St Thomas points out that Baptism of desire takes the place of Baptism of water only when circumstances exclude the receiving of the sacrament. Otherwise, the Lord Jesus has established the rule that Baptism of water is necessary for salvation. But babies being aborted *are* in a situation in which they are prevented from receiving the sacrament of Baptism.

(e) St Thomas avers that salvation is available in some way at every age in the life of every human individual. But living in the womb *is* an age in the life of every human individual, since human embryos and human fetuses are already human individuals endowed with a human soul and with the faculties of intelligence and free will. Therefore, salvation must in some way be available to them, especially if they are facing death in the womb. But Baptism of water is not available, and so, some other means of salvation must be at hand.

(f) St Thomas maintains that, since 'it is in the power of a man to impede another man from being baptized with water', therefore, 'there can be salvation even without Baptism of water by faith and contrition alone.' But babies being killed in the womb are being prevented by the power of man from ever receiving Baptism of water. And, as innocent children, they have no need of contrition, while their faith can be supplied from the faith of the Church. Therefore, sanctification should in some way be available to them.

(g) No one deserves sanctifying grace and no one merits the first grace, but the only great obstacle to the merciful love of Jesus is bad will, and St Thomas assures us that babies in the womb 'do not have an inordinate act of the will'. Hence, they are fully disposed for an infusion of sanctifying grace, either directly by Christ or indirectly through the ministry of others. St Thomas also teaches that, since original sin is in children, it is needful that some remedy be available to them, and he goes on to say that 'whoever denies that Baptism can be afforded to little children is denying the divine mercy'. Hence, one might equally argue that whoever denies that sanctification is in some way available to children being aborted from the womb is denying the divine mercy.

(h) St Thomas maintains that children in their mothers' wombs cannot be subjected to the physical or the mental acts of human beings in such wise as to be administered the sacraments of salvation, although they can, 'by a privilege of grace,' be sanctified by the work of God, 'outside of the common law', as though miraculously, 'as is evident from those who have been sanctified in the womb'. It seems that St Thomas is here referring to a general law laid down by Jesus and cited by St Augustine to the effect that children who are going to be born are not to be baptized until they are actually born. However, this law would not seem to apply to children who will never be born. And thus St Thomas can also say that 'if a mother should die while a child is living in her womb, the womb should be opened and the child should be baptized.' But not without hesitation does St Thomas venture to claim that a child in his mother's womb cannot be cleansed from original sin by any act of man, whether physical or mental, for he adds 'as far as human knowledge can tell'. In this he is relying partly upon the medical knowledge available in his time. Modern medicine can reach the child physically in the womb.[86]

(i) St Thomas explains that, when children are being baptized, 'it does not matter what the intention is of those who are carrying them', because children intend and believe through the faith of the Church. Hence, the murder of an infant in the womb can be received as a martyrdom.

(j) St Thomas notes with the Church (cf. *CCC* 1257) that it is Christ who principally baptizes, but the Lord did not limit his saving power to the sacraments. We know of the willingness of Jesus to let the little children come unto him (Mark 10:14). Now, St Thomas points out that circumcision was an efficacious sign of healing from original sin, not least in the shedding of the blood of an infant, 'in which is signified the Passion of Christ'. Why, then, would Jesus not see, in the putting to death of an infant *in the womb*, a sign of his own Passion, and so administer to the child, either directly or through others, his healing and saving grace?

(k) St Thomas recalls that the children of the ancients 'were saved in the faith of their parents' or of some other believing adult. St Thomas does not include children in the womb in this operation of faith, which, he says, 'had the sacramental power which Baptism of water has now'. However, he was not adverting to the special case of infants being killed in the womb. Now, the virtue of Christian faith is not weaker after the coming of Christ that it was before. Why, therefore, can we not believe with grounded hope that Jesus will use the faith of his Church, and in particular the charity of Blessed Mary and of the saints along with the fervour of his faithful on earth, to sanctify these victimized babies? This would be an act of living faith, not having the sacramental power of Baptism, but having intercessory power with the Heart of Jesus.

(l) St Thomas allows that, as at Sodom, little children – even children in the womb – may be temporally punished for the sins of their parents, but he does not say that they may be *eternally* punished for their parents' sins. Yet to be deprived of Heaven because of the sin of one's First Parents would be an eternal penalty that St Thomas does not seem to envisage here. Nor does St Thomas anywhere visualize anyone being punished for sins that he would have committed in other circumstances, but never actually carried out.

(m) St Thomas gives reasons why, under the Old Law, circumcision was given to males as a remedy for original sin, but not to females, and he points out that male infants who were faced with death before their eighth day of birth could be saved eternally by an act of faith on the part of their parents. But he says nothing specifically about how female infants could be saved, and yet it is contrary to the tenor of his thought to assume that he visualized no ordinary means of salvation for females throughout the entire period of the Old Testament. Similarly, it is reasonable to assume that, while St Thomas does not speak specifically about a remedy for original sin in infants being murdered in the womb, his general principles would allow for some ordinary means of salvation for these infants, over and above a rare direct sanctification by Jesus alone.

Infants being aborted are a special object of divine mercy for at least two reasons: they are absolutely free of personal sin, even though they are stained with original sin, and they are being murdered by their own parents. Now, being murdered by one's own parents is a sin against the natural law that cries out to Heaven. Since Jesus, our Saviour, 'will have all men to be saved and to come to the knowledge of the truth' (1 Tim. 2:4), he also wants children undergoing deadly assault in the womb to be saved and to come to the knowledge of the truth, the truth that he *is*. The Blessed Virgin Mary, as the new Eve, the Mother of Jesus and the Mother of the Church, is also the Advocate, Helper, Benefactress, and Mediatrix of babies being attacked in the womb. In fact, we might say, every time the knife of an abortionist pierces one of their hearts, a sword of sorrow pierces her heart (cf. Luke 2:35). Seeing them dying in the state of original sin, will she not say once again to her divine Son, 'they have no wine' (John 2:3). If Jesus willed to convert the heart of Saul, who 'persecuted the Church of God' (1 Cor. 15:9), into Paul the Apostle and martyr, if Jesus, looking with pity upon a dying thief on Calvary, 'turned a penalty for murder into a martyrdom', will he refuse to convert the tiny hearts of these innocent victims into confessors of his mercy? If Isaac signified Christ in that he was being offered in sacrifice to God, why would Jesus not see in the deliberate killing of a human fetus a representation of his own death on Calvary?

All children in the womb have guardian angels, since 'human life from its very beginning ("*inde ab initio*") until death is in their care and is surrounded by their intercession' (*CCC*, no. 336). But when do children need the care and intercession of their guardian angels more than at the moment in which they are being assaulted to the point of death itself in the womb? And Angels can sanctify (cf. Isa. 6:7), when commissioned by God to do so.

Of course, Lazarus was carried by Angels to Abraham's bosom (Luke 16:22), that is, to the Limbo of the Fathers, but this was only a temporary waiting place until Jesus should open the door to Heaven. Now that Jesus has opened the door to Heaven, are we to suppose the guardian angels drop off the souls of aborted children in the Limbo of Children as they themselves proceed on their way back to Heaven? It does not seem so. Jesus says: 'He that shall receive one such little child in my name receives me' (Matt. 18:5). Therefore, conversely, whoever kills one such little child in opposition to the will of Jesus (Mark 10:19) is killing Jesus. And Jesus also said: 'their angels in Heaven always see the face of my Father who is in Heaven' (Matt. 18:10). Does there not seem to be a hint in these words that, if a little child is killed in the womb in contempt of his vocation to see forever the Face of God in Heaven, the angels will, nevertheless, carry the soul of that little child to Heaven, 'for the Son of Man is come to save that which is lost' (Matt. 18:11).

Conclusion

St Thomas, while he assumed that aborted children die in original sin unless they are sanctified in some way apart from Baptism of water, also enuntiated various facts and principles which support the hope that aborted babies are sanctified at the moment of their death. These elements include such things as the martyrdom of infants, the vicarious faith of the Church, the availability of sanctification at every age of the human individual, sanctification in the womb, and sanctification by Jesus directly or through the ministry of Angels.

The Church, in the growing awareness of the merciful love of Jesus and the maternal love of Mary, has tended more and more to manifest her hope for the salvation of unbaptized babies. In view of John 3:5, the Church cannot guarantee this, and she must insist that infants be baptized at the earliest reasonable moment after their birth. But aborted babies are a special case. And so, considering the special reasons pertaining to this case as reviewed in the present article, and relying on a wider interpretation of Matthew 2:18 and Jeremiah 31:16, together with Luke 23:43, Luke 2:35, Genesis 3:15, Apocalypse 12:17; Apocalypse 7:14, and a multitude of supporting Scriptural texts, I conclude, subject to the final judgment of the Church, that the Magisterium could proclaim all infants murdered in the womb to be companion martyrs of the Holy Innocents of Bethlehem, cleansed and sanctified at the moment of their death in the redemptive Blood of Christ.

Notes

[1] Congregation for the Doctrine of the Faith, *Donum vitae*, I. 1.

[2] R. Lawler, D. Wuerl, and T. Lawler (eds.), *The Teaching of Christ* (Huntington, Ind: Our Sunday Visitor, 1976), p. 529.

[3] Cf. J. Pohle, 'Pelagius and Pelagianism', *The Catholic Encyclopaedia*, vol. 11 (New York: Encyclopaedia Press, 1911), p. 607A.

[4] Pope Pius XII, Discourse of 29 October, 1951.

[5] Alphonsus Liguori, *Theologia Moralis*, Bk. 6, tract. 2, ch 1, no. 97.

[6] Congregation for the Doctrine of the Faith, *Pastoralis actio*, art. 13.

[7] *Roman Catechism*, Part II, 'Baptism'.

[8] Aquinas, *De Malo*, q. 5 art. 2 corp. et ad 1.

9 For a brief history of this theological discussion, see P. J. Toner, 'Limbo', *The Catholic Encyclopedia*, vol. 9 (New York: Encyclopaedia Press, 1909), pp. 256–259.

10 Aquinas, *In IV Sent.*, dist. 43 q. 1 art. 1b = *S. Th.*, Suppl. q. 75 art. 2.

11 Augustine, *De civitate Dei*, bk. 20, ch. 23.

12 Aquinas, *S. Th.*, III q. 61, art. 1, corp. and ad 3.

13 Aquinas, *S. Th.*, III q. 62, art. 5, ad 2.

14 Aquinas, *S. Th.*, III q. 68, art. 9, corp.

15 Aquinas, *S. Th.*, III q. 69, art. 2, corp.

16 Aquinas, *S. Th.*, III q. 49, art. 5, corp.

17 Aquinas, *S. Th.*, III q. 66, art. 11, tit. and corp.

18 Augustine, *De Baptismo contra Donatistas*, bk. 4, ch. 22: PL Vol. 43, col. 173.

19 Aquinas, *S. Th.*, III q. 66, art. 11, corp.

20 Aquinas, *S. Th.*, III q. 68, art. 1, corp.

21 Aquinas, *S. Th.*, III q. 66, art. 3, ad 3.

22 Aquinas, *S. Th.*, III q. 66, art. 12, corp.

23 Aquinas, *S. Th.*, III q. 68, art. 2, corp.

24 Aquinas, *S. Th.*, III q. 68, art. 2, ad 1.

25 Aquinas, *S. Th.*, III q. 68, art. 2, ad 3.

26 Aquinas, *S. Th.*, III q. 61, art. 4, corp.

27 Aquinas, *S. Th.*, III q. 69, art. 5, corp.

28 Aquinas, *S. Th.*, III q. 69, art. 5, ad 1.

29 Aquinas, *In IV Sent.*, dist. 4, q. 3, art. 3e, ad 1.

30 Aquinas, *S. Th.*, III q. 61, art. 3, corp.

31 Aquinas, *S. Th.*, III q. 62, art. 6, corp.

32 Aquinas, *S. Th.*, III q. 62, art. 6, ad 3.

33 Aquinas, *In IV Sent.*, dist. 1, q. 1, art. 2d.

34 Aquinas, *In IV Sent.*, dist. 1, q. 2, art. 1a

35 Aquinas, *In IV Sent.*, dist. 1, q. 2, art. 4c

36 Aquinas, *In IV Sent.*, dist. 1, q. 2, art. 5a.

37 Aquinas, *S. Th.* III q. 70 art. 4 corp.

38 Aquinas, *In IV Sent.* dist. 1, q. 2, art. 4b.

39 Gregory the Great, *Moralia in Job*, PL Vol. 75, col. 635B.

40 Aquinas, *S. Th.* III q. 68, art. 1, ad 1.

41 Aquinas, *S. Th.* III q. 70, art. 4, ad 2.

42 Gregory the Great *Moralia in Job*, bk. 4, ch. 3 PL Vol. 75, col. 635B.

43 Aquinas, *S. Th.* II–II q. 85, art. 1 ad 2.

44 Aquinas, *S. Th.* III q. 68, art. 10, corp.

45 Aquinas, *S. Th.* III q. 70, art. 4, ad 3.

46 Aquinas, *S. Th.* III q. 70, art. 2 and 4.

47 Aquinas, *In IV Sent.*, dist. 1, art. 6c, sed contra.

48 Aquinas, *In IV Sent.*, dist. 1, q. 2 art. 6a, corp.

49 Aquinas, *In IV Sent.*, dist. 1, q. 2 art. 6b, corp.

50 Aquinas, *In IV Sent.*, dist. 4, q. 3 art. 3b, ad 3.

51 Aquinas, *In IV Sent.*, dist. 4, q. 3 art. 3b, ob 3.

52 Aquinas, *In IV Sent.*, dist. 4, q. 3 art. 3b, sed contra 1.

53 Aquinas, *In IV Sent.*, dist. 4, q. 3 art. 3b, corp.
54 Aquinas, *In IV Sent.*, dist. 4, q. 3 art. 3b, ad 3.
55 Aquinas, *S. Th.* III q. 68, art. 10.
56 Aquinas, *S. Th.* III q. 67, art. 4, corp.
57 Aquinas, *S. Th.* III q. 67, art. 5, ad 1.
58 Aquinas, *S. Th.* III q. 67, art. 5, ad 2.
59 Aquinas, *S. Th.* III q. 64, art. 3, ad 4.
60 Aquinas, *In IV Sent.*, dist. 4, q. 3, art. 3d, ex.
61 Aquinas, *S. Th.* III q. 64, art. 7, corp.
62 Aquinas, *S. Th.* III q. 64, art. 7, ad 1.
63 Aquinas, *S. Th.* III q. 68, art. 11, ad 1.
64 Aquinas, *In IV Sent.*, dist. 6, q. 1, art. 1c, sed contra 2.
65 Aquinas, *In IV Sent.*, dist. 6, q. 1, art. 1b, corp.
66 Aquinas, *In IV Sent.*, dist. 1, q. 2, art. 6b, ad 2.
67 Aquinas, *In IV Sent.*, dist. 6, q. 1, art. 1a, ad 2.
68 Aquinas, *S. Th.*, II–II q. 108, art. 4, ad 3.
69 Aquinas, *In IV Sent.*, dist. 4, q. 3 art. 1a, corp.
70 Aquinas, *S. Th.*, III q. 68, art. 11, sed contra and corp.
71 Aquinas *S. Th.*, III q. 68, art. 11, ad 2.
72 Aquinas, *In IV Sent* dist 6 q. 1, art. 1a, corp.
73 Augustine, *Epistola* 187, PL Vol. 33, col. 844.
74 Aquinas, *S. Th.*, III q. 68, art. 11, sed contra.
75 Aquinas, *S. Th.*, III q. 68, art. 11, ad 3.
76 Aquinas, *In IV Sent.*, dist. 4, q. 3 art. 1c, ad 3.
77 Aquinas, *De Malo* q. 5 art. 3, corp.
78 Aquinas, *S. Th.* III q. 68, art. 9, ad 1.
79 Aquinas, *S. Th.* III q. 68, art. 9, ad 2.
80 Augustine, *Epistola ad Bonifacium*, PL Vol. 33, col. 362.
81 Aquinas, *S. Th.* III q. 68, art. 9, ad 2.
82 Aquinas, *S. Th.* III q. 64, art. 1, ad 2.
83 Aquinas, *S. Th.* III q. 69, art. 6, ad 3.
84 Aquinas, *S. Th.* III q. 69, art. 8, corp.
85 Aquinas, *S. Th.* III q. 69, art. 6, ad 4: quoting Augustine: PL 33 361.
86 Alphonsus Liguori, *Theologia moralis*, bk 6, tract 2, cf. 1, no. 107.

Index